W9-ACC-593

YOU CAN TEACH YOURSELF®
GUITAR

By William Bay

> *You Can Teach Yourself®Guitar* is a new concept in guitar literature. It is an excellent method designed for any student who wants to learn the basics of playing the guitar. Upon completion of this method, the student will be well versed in a variety of keys and accompaniment styles. The guitar is truly a fun instrument. This text should open a world of creative possibilities to the guitar student.

A stero cassette tape, compact disc, VHS video, and CD ROM of the music in this book are now available. The publisher strongly recommends the use of one of these resources along with the text to insure accuracy of interpretation and ease in learning.

Visit us on the Web at http://www.melbay.com — E-mail us at email@melbay.com

TYPES OF GUITARS

Classic

Standard Folk

Jumbo Folk

12-String

Arch-Top

Solid-Body Electric

Acoustic Electric

CLASSIC GUITAR—The classic guitar is characterized by the round sound hole, nylon or gut strings, and a rather wide neck. The reason for the wide neck is to allow the right-hand fingers to fit in between the strings for fingerstyle playing. The wood on a classic guitar is usually lighter than on a regular folk-style guitar in order to bring out the delicate tone of the nylon strings. Never put metal strings on a guitar made for nylon strings. The wood will not be able to stand the increased stress. We usually recommend starting on nylon strings, as they are easier (less painful) on the fingers.

STANDARD FOLK GUITAR—This is a very widely used guitar today. It may be played with the fingers or with a pick. It is characterized by a round sound hole and a more narrow neck than is found on the "classic"-type guitars. The narrow neck is easier to finger barre or more complicated chords on. Ball-end nylon strings may usually be put on this type of guitar; however, since it is made for steel strings, it will not produce a tone with nylon comparable to a guitar made for nylon. It is a good rule to stick with whatever type of strings the guitar was originally made for (i.e., nylon or metal). This type of guitar puts out considerably more volume than a nylon-stringed or classical guitar.

JUMBO FOLK GUITAR—This style of guitar is similar to the standar folk guitar except, of course, for the larger body. While the large body on this type is bulkier to handle, a fuller and deeper tone results from it. A fuller volume range can be obtained from this style of guitar than from a standard folk model. Some jumbo models come with a wide neck comparable to that found on a classic guitar. This is advantageous to the player who devotes most of his playing to fingerstyle. Standard folk guitars and jumbo folk guitars are sometimes referred to as "flat-top" guitars due to the flat surface on the face of the guitar (containing the round sound hole).

TWELVE-STRING GUITAR—The 12-string guitar has a large body which is similar to a jumbo model. The neck is wider in order to comfortably fit all 12 strings. The guitar is played like a regular 6-string model since the strings are tuned to the same notes. On a 12-string guitar there are six sets of strings, two strings to a set. Each set is tuned to the corresponding set on a 6-string guitar; however, some sets may have an octave spread. While this style of guitar is excellent for folk and blues playing, it is bulkier and less mobile technically. It is not recommended, therefore, that a student begin with this type of guitar.

ARCH-TOP—This type of guitar gets its name from the curved (arched) top on the instrument. Both the front and back of this type of guitar are arched. Modern arch-top guitars contain "F"-shaped sound holes. The curvature of the front and back lend a degree of mellowness to the sound. The "F" holes tend to project the sound for greater distances than a comparable round-hole model. Arch-top guitars find much usage as rhythm instruments in dance bands and in country music. Most folk and fingerstyle players prefer the immediate full spread of sound found on round-hole models. Arch-top guitars have metal strings.

SOLID-BODY ELECTRIC—This is the type of guitar found in most of today's rock music. It is built for speed and amplification. The sound possibilities are endless, depending on the pick-up, tone, and amplifier combination chosen. It is usually cheaper and more practical to begin on a non-electric (acoustic) model.

ACOUSTIC ELECTRIC—This type of guitar is also found in much of today's rock music. Again, the sound possibilities vary according to the electric components selected. Many jazz guitarists prefer an acoustic electric with a deep body. (Essentially this is an arch-top guitar with an electric pick-up mounted on it.) A mellow tone can result from this combination, but the type of electrical pick-up and amplifier influence this.

THE GUITAR AND ITS PARTS

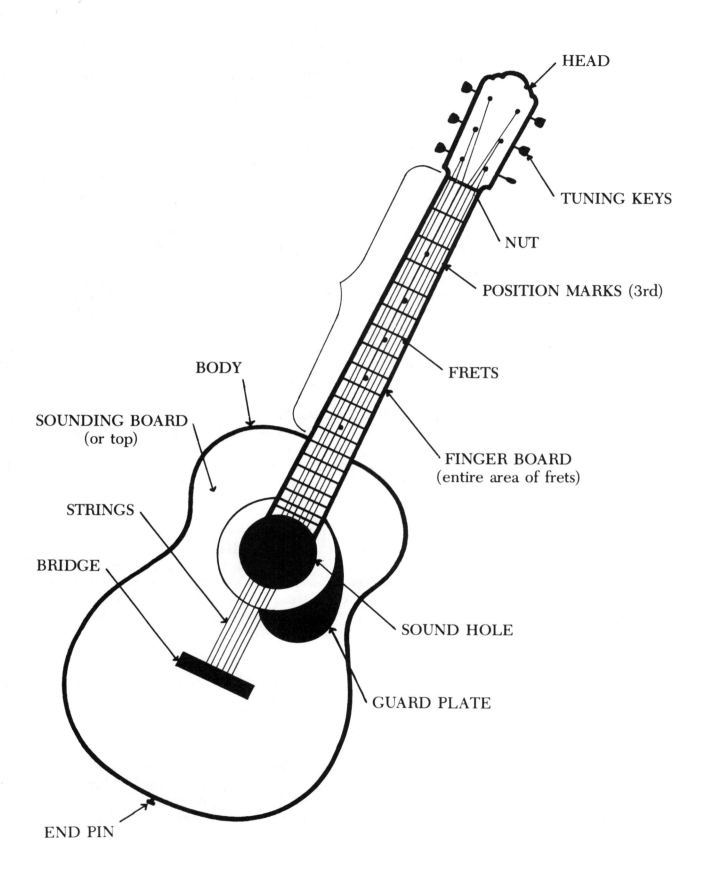

HEAD

TUNING KEYS

NUT

POSITION MARKS (3rd)

FRETS

FINGER BOARD
(entire area of frets)

BODY

SOUNDING BOARD
(or top)

STRINGS

BRIDGE

SOUND HOLE

GUARD PLATE

END PIN

HOW TO BUY A GUITAR

The type of guitar you buy depends to a degree on what style of music you wish to play. Generally, for purposes of beginning, we recommend a classic-model guitar (round hole with nylon strings). Usually the nylon strings are more comfortable for beginners' tender fingers. Be careful that the size of the guitar is neither too big and unwieldy nor too small. It should feel comfortable to you.

WHERE TO BUY—Any reputable music merchant should handle a wide enough selection of guitars to choose from. We do advise you to choose a merchant who has the ability and facility to service your instrument. Adjustments and minor repairs are frequently necessary, so be sure your dealer can give you service. You might also inquire into renting an instrument, as many music merchants have very reasonable rental programs. Do make certain, however, that the rented instrument is comfortable to play. Finally, you might investigate what is available in the way of a used guitar. Many good buys are available in used instruments. Again, make certain that the guitar in question meets your needs as a beginner. You don't need the most expensive instrument to begin.

WHAT TO LOOK FOR—The main requisite for a beginner's guitar is ease of playing. Make sure it is comfortable. If there are several models to choose from, listen to them and compare the tones. Most people prefer a guitar with a deeper and more mellow sound. Look out for neck warpage. Some guitars do have warped necks. Usually, if this is the case, the neck is bowed back and the strings half way down the neck are disproportionately high off the fingerboard. When a reverse warp is present the strings will at some point be too close to the fingerboard, and somewhere on up the fingerboard a buzz will occur. Look out also for a nut that is too high. (Refer back to the diagram showing the parts of the guitar.) When the nut is too high, the strings will be hard to press down in the first fret. This problem can be corrected easily by filing down the grooves holding the strings. The dealer should make this adjustment. Be careful that the strings are not lowered enough to cause a buzz. Most important of all, go to a reputable music merchant who stands behind and services the products he sells.

CASES—Most guitars come in a vinyl bag, cardboard case, or plywood case. The case you buy should reflect the amount of protection you wish to give your instrument. The plywood case is the best; however, they are expensive and not necessary for some beginner models. Both the vinyl bag and the pressboard case do an adequate job. The price of the case should not exceed the value of your instrument. No case can work miracles. If you drop your guitar, regardless of the type of case, you are likely to crack it. Buy a case that will give you adequate protection from bumps, kicks, and moisture. With any instrument, a good case is a worthwhile investment.

CARE OF YOUR GUITAR

The better your guitar, usually speaking, the older and more fragile are the woods. Try to keep your guitar from extreme temperature and sudden changes in temperature. Do not place it in the sun, by a heat vent or radiator, by an air conditioner, or leave it in the trunk of a car. Watch out for bumps, kicks, and dropping your guitar. If you use a strap to hold it, make certain that both the strap and the strap button to which it is attached are of sufficient strength. If you guitar needs a strap button, let your dealer install it for you.

Be careful of buttons and belt buckles. They can destroy the back finish of a guitar. Make certain that the guitar has the proper strings. (Don't put metal strings on a guitar made to hold nylon!) Make sure that your instrument isn't tuned too high. If in doubt, tune it to an "in-tune" piano or go to your local music store and purchase a guitar pitch pipe. Finally, an occasional polishing will keep the finish on your instrument bright. Again, you can obtain guitar polish at your local music store.

STRINGS

There are many types of strings on the market today; so many, in fact, that the beginning student may become quite confused by it all. Below we attempt to clarify some of the types and uses of strings.

NYLON STRINGS—Nylon strings are found on classic guitars. This type of string has a soft, mellow tone and is easy on the fingers. This is a very good string with which to begin. Certain problems occur with tuning a new set of nylon strings. When they are new, they stretch quite a bit and therefore need frequent tuning. They settle down after a day or so. The tone of nylon strings is brought out best by thin, aged woods (usually rosewood back and sides and spruce top). Nylon strings lose some of their vibrance when put on a guitar made originally for metal strings. (The wood on this type of guitar is thicker and stronger to take the stress of metal strings.)

BALL-END NYLON—These nylon strings have balls on the ends similar to those found on metal strings. They are usually a little heavier than regular nylon and can take vigorous strumming. They are frequently called "folk nylon," as they are the best type of nylon string for folk playing. The balls on the ends enable them to fit on a standard folk guitar, which holds the strings by means of pegs in the bridge. No nylon string will last long if attached to a metal tail piece. Usually the top three strings of ball-end nylon sets are black nylon, and the bottom three have a brass wrapping.

MONEL—Monel string are steel strings. Metal strings have a much sharper and louder tone than nylon. Monel strings are steel gray in color. The thickness varies according to the type of set purchased. For beginners we recommend a medium light gauge set. This would have the following gauges per string:

E or 1st—.010-.012	G or 3rd—.020-.024 (wound)	A or 5th—.038-.044
B or 2nd—.012-.016	D or 4th—.026-.032	E or 6th—.048-.054

SILK-AND-STEEL—Silk-and-steel sets are a very flexible metal compound. They are bright silver in color and have a softer tone than most other metal strings. They are excellent for fingerstyle playing. Also, they are usually easier on the fingers than some of the harder, more brittle types. If you are using metal strings and are experiencing sore fingers, you might try a set of silk-and-steel! Silk-and-steel sets will not pick up electrically and should not be used on electric guitars.

STRINGS (CONT'D.)

BRONZE—Bronze strings are made of a bronze alloy and have a rather pronounced, striking tone. They are excellent for folk and jumbo models needing volume and brilliance of sound. They come in light, medium, and heavy gauges. Usually the light gauges are preferable for a fingerstyle player, while the medium and heavy gauge sets lend themselves suitably to the "hard-strummin' pick player." Bronze strings are not for the solid-body electric guitar.

BRASS—Brass strings are very similar to bronze sets in usage. The brass string is usually a little more brittle than the bronze string, and the tone is a little more sharp or harsh (depending upon your personal taste and interpretation). These strings also are not for the solid-body electric guitar.

FLAT-POLISHED—Flat-polished strings are monel strings which have been ground so that the surface is smooth. (The little ridges are taken out.) These strings come for both acoustic and electric guitars. They have the advantage of being easier on the fingers. Technically, some guitarists claim greater left-hand velocity using a flat-polished string. These sets still retain the tonal quality of a standard, round-wound string.

FLAT-WOUND—Flat-wound strings are for the electric guitar. They are wound flat (no ridges) and are made of some monel or nickel compound. They differ from flat-polished strings in that they are wound flat from the beginning. Flat-polished strings are round wound and then ground flat. Flat-wound strings are very comfortable to the left hand and give a smooth bell-like tone when amplified. This string is preferred by many jazz guitarists.

GENERAL COMMENTS—The string selected depends on the type of guitar you play, the style of music you prefer, the sound you want to create, and your preferences for comfort and ease of playing. As you can see, there are many variables; and it is a highly personal decision. Do not leave strings on your instrument too long. When a string gets old it sounds dead and loses its flexibility. Just how long to keep a set of strings depends on how much the instrument is played, the temperature and humidity, the actual physical chemistry of an individual's hand perspiration, and the quality of the set of strings. We are hesitant to give a standard rule for changing strings; however, beginning students probably can start looking and listening for wear at about five weeks. Again, when in doubt, ask your teacher. Strings can be purchased at any local music store.

HOW TO HOLD THE GUITAR

Fig. 1

Fig. 2

Fig. 3

Fig. 4

Fig. 5

First, hold the guitar as shown in Figure 1. Next, bring it in close to the body as shown in Figure 2. Then, move your right hand as shown in the position in Figure 3. This will bring the guitar firmly against your body. The left hand is then moved, as shown in Figure 4, up into the area of first position. This is where the first finger is resting in the middle of the first fret. Finally, Figure 5 shows the right hand getting ready to strum the strings of the guitar.

THE LEFT HAND

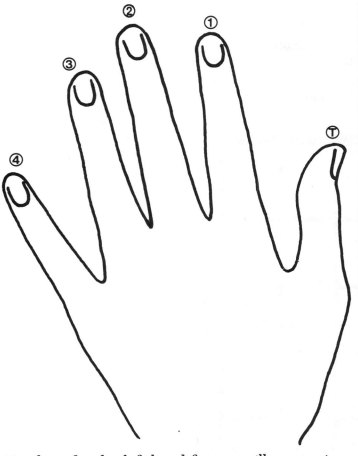

Numbers for the left hand fingers will appear in chord diagrams throughout the book.

LEFT HAND POSITION

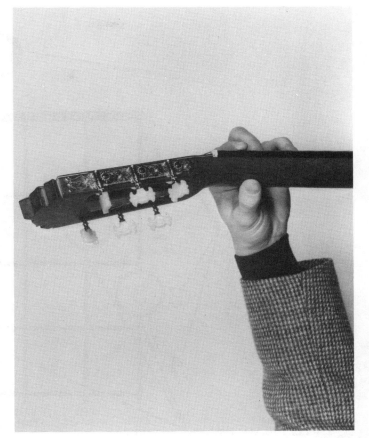

Fig. 6

LEFT HAND POSITION

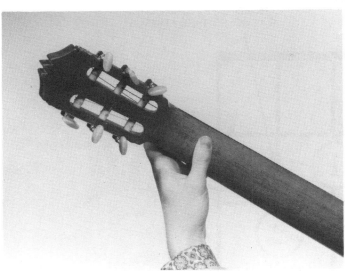

Fig. 7

Fig. 8

To begin with, keep the left elbow and wrist relaxed. Avoid positioning that strains and tightens your left wrist and elbow. The important thing to remember is to place the left hand so that the hand is arched and so that the fingers can fall straight down on the strings. Greater technique can be obtained by pressing down the strings with the tips of the fingers than with the fleshy part.

EXPLANATION OF CHORD SYMBOLS

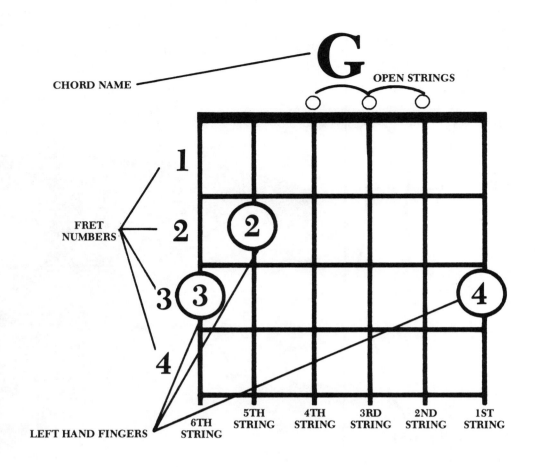

CHORD NAME

G

OPEN STRINGS

FRET NUMBERS

1

2 ②

3 ③ ④

4

LEFT HAND FINGERS

6TH STRING · 5TH STRING · 4TH STRING · 3RD STRING · 2ND STRING · 1ST STRING

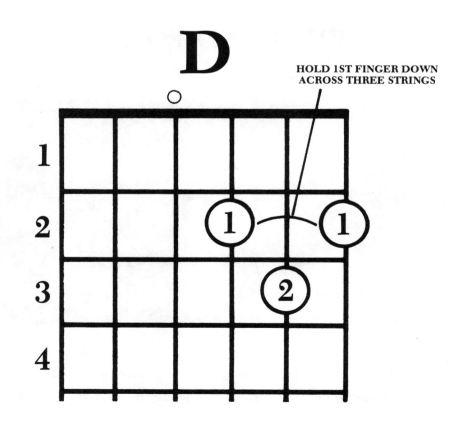

D

HOLD 1ST FINGER DOWN ACROSS THREE STRINGS

1

2 ① ①

3 ②

4

TUNING THE GUITAR

The six open strings of the guitar will be of the same pitch as the six notes shown in the illustration of the piano keyboard. Note that five of the strings are below the middle C of the piano keyboard.

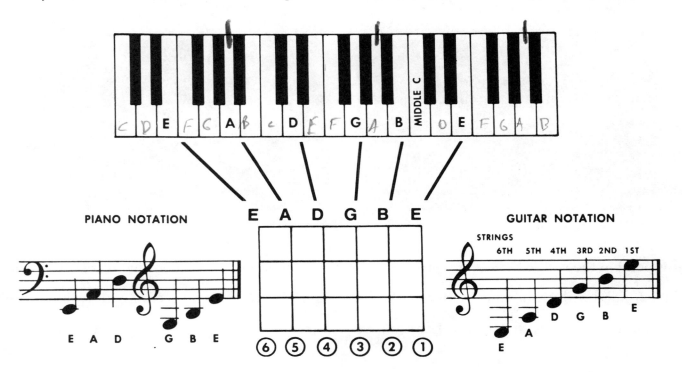

PIANO NOTATION

E A D G B E

GUITAR NOTATION

E A D G B E

E A D G B E

⑥ ⑤ ④ ③ ② ①

ANOTHER METHOD OF TUNING

1. Tune the 6th string in unison to the E or twelfth white key to the LEFT of MIDDLE C on the piano.

2. Place the finger behind the fifth fret of the 6th string. this will give you the tone or pitch of the 5th string. (A)

3. Place finger behind the fifth fret of the 5th string to get the pitch of the 4th string. (D)

4. Repeat same procedure to obtain the pitch of the 3rd string. (G)

5. Place finger behind the FOURTH FRET of the 3rd string to get the pitch of the 2nd string. (B)

6. Place finger behind the fifth fret of the 2nd string to get the pitch of the 1st string. (E)

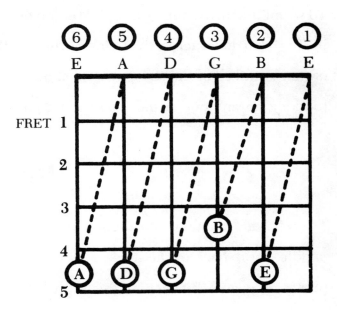

PITCH PIPES

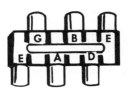

Pitch pipes with instructions for their usage may be obtained at any music store. Each pipe will have the correct pitch of each guitar string and are recommended to be used when a piano is not available.

STRUMMING THE STRINGS
RIGHT HAND PLACEMENT

Fig. 9

Fig. 10

At this point in the student's learning process we will be concentrating on coordinating chord fingering in the left hand with strumming motion in the right hand. We, therefore, recommend strumming with the thumb down across the strings. Later on we will introduce the possible use of a pick.

To strum the instrument, place the thumb by the sixth string. This is the largest of the six strings (figure 9). To strum down across the strings, bring the thumb down gently across all six strings. Do this a number of times until all of the strings sound at once. The strum should be even and the thumb should not rest too long on any one string. You should glide evenly across all six strings (figure 10).

REMEMBER

The left hand should be positioned on the neck of the guitar so that the thumb rests comfortably in the middle of the back of the neck. This will require you to arch your hand somewhat. Look again at the photos on page 9. By keeping the left hand thumb in the middle of the neck, and by learning to play in this fashion from the beginning, your fingers will have the tendency to come down directly on top of the strings and avoid the problems of accidently laying across the wrong strings when you finger notes and chords. When you lay your fingers across the wrong string, you will accidently deaden the sound of some of the notes. Proper positioning of the left hand will give you great freedom in fingering rapid passages later on. Also, by placing the thumb in the middle of the neck, you are providing maximum strength in fingering difficult chords.

G CHORD—EZ FORM

× = means do not play

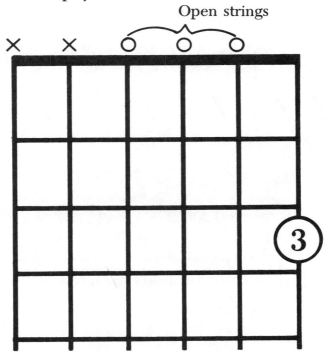

× = Do not play 6th & 5th strings
○ = 4th, 3rd, & 2nd strings are played open
③ = Press the 3rd finger down on the 3rd fret on the 1st string

TIME SIGNATURES

/ = down strum—from large strings to small

$\frac{4}{4}$ or C = COMMON TIME

4 strums or beats per measure

Hold the G chord and play it in this manner.

$\frac{4}{4}$ G / / / / | G / / / / | G / / / / | G / / / / ‖

$\frac{3}{4}$ = THREE-FOUR or WALTZ TIME

3 strums or beats per measure

Hold the G chord and play it in the following manner.

$\frac{3}{4}$ G / / / | G / / / | G / / / | G / / / ‖

$\frac{2}{4}$ = TWO-FOUR TIME

2 strums or beats per measure

Play it in this manner.

$\frac{2}{4}$ G / / | G / / | G / / | G / / ‖

Strumming The G Chord

╱ = Down strum - From large strings to small

Brother John Sing & Play

Starting Pitch

Student

Are you sleep-ing? Are you sleep-ing? Bro-ther John. Bro-ther John.

Morn-ing bells are ring-ing! Morn-ing bells are ring-ing! Din-dan-don. Din-dan-don.

C Chord-EZ Form

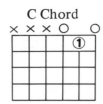

C Chord
× × × O   O
①

Play only the top 3 strings!

Make sure your 1st finger
does not accidentally rest
against the 1st string!

Three Blind Mice

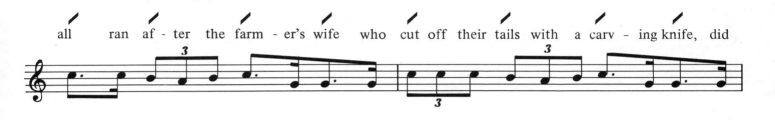

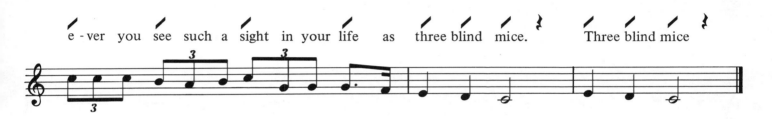

Row, Row, Row Your Boat

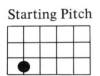

This means 2 strums or beats per measure

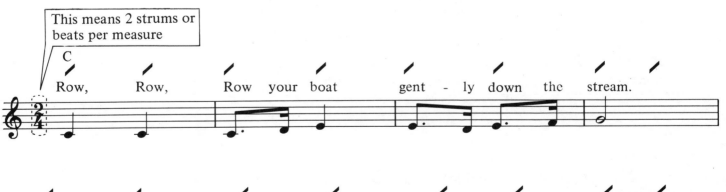

G7 Chord—EZ Form

G7 Chord

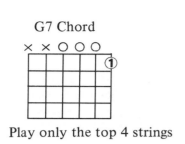

Play only the top 4 strings

G7

C   G7   C   G7

C   G7   C   G7   C

Starting Pitch

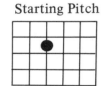

Skip To My Lou

C
Choose your part-ner   skip to my Lou,
G7
Choose your part-ner   skip to my Lou,

C
Choose your part-ner   skip to my Lou,
G7   C
Skip to my Lou my   dar - ling!

C   G7
Left and Right,   Oh skip to my Lou   Left and Right,   Oh skip to my Lou
C   G7   C
Left and Right,   Oh skip to my Lou   Skip to my Lou my darling.

Rock-A-My Soul

Spiritual

Starting Pitch

C

Rock - a - my soul____ in the bo - som of A - bra - ham;

G7

Rock a - my-soul__ in the bo-som of A - bra-ham; Rock-a-my soul in the

C

bo-som of A - bra-ham; Oh, Rock-a my soul._____

G7   C

Polly Wolly Doodle

Starting Pitch

C

Oh I went down South for to see my Sal, sing-ing pol-ly wol-ly doo-dle all the

G7

day, My Sal she is a pret - ty gal, sing-ing

C

pol-ly wol-ly doo-dle all the day. Fare thee well,__ fare thee well, fare thee

G7   G7

well my fair - y fey, For I'm goin'- to Lou - si - an - a for to

C

see my Su - si - an - na, Sing-ing pol - ly wol - ly doo-dle all the day.

19

THE FULL G CHORD

If your "E-Z" form of the G chord is sounding clear, you are ready to try the full G chord. Note the change in fingering. Practice to make sure your fingers aren't touching and deadening the wrong strings.

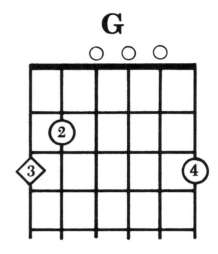

G

Diamond will be bass note. Fourth finger is used on the top string because it will enable quicker transition to G7 and C chords.

To play the full G chord—Make certain that your left-hand thumb is placed in the middle of the back of the neck. Bring your fingers directly down on the strings. Practice to make sure your fingers aren't touching and deadening the wrong strings.

THE FULL C CHORD

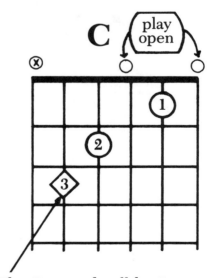

C play open

The Diamond will be Bass note.

Remember that the three basic chords in the key of G are: G, C, and D7.

Oh, My Darling Clementine

Starting Pitch

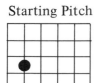

Putting On The Style

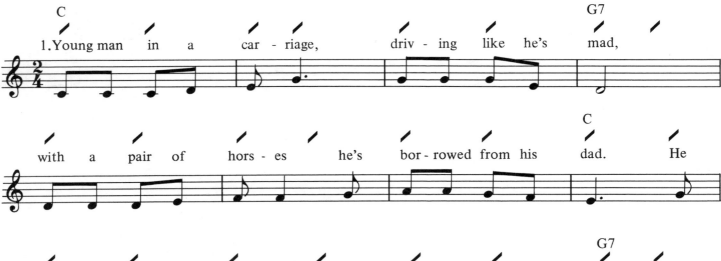

1. Young man in a carriage, driving like he's mad,
with a pair of horses he's borrowed from his dad. He
cracks his whip so lively, just to make the ladies smile,
but they know he's only putting on the style.

Chorus:
C
Putting on the agony,
G7
Putting on the style,
That's what all the young folks
C
Are doing all the while.
And as I look around me
G7
I'm very apt to smile,
To see so many people
C   G7   C
Putting on the style.

C
2. Sweet sixteen and goes to church,
G7
Just to see the boys,
Laughs and giggles
C
At every little noise.
She turns this way a little,
G7
And turns that way a while,
But everybody knows she's only
C   G7   C
Putting on the style.
Chorus

C
3. Young man just from college
G7
Makes a big display
With a great big jawbreak,
C
Which he can hardly say.
It can't be found in Webster's,
G7
And won't be for a while,
But everybody knows he's only
C   G7   C
Putting on the style.
Chorus

Three Fishermen

Starting Pitch

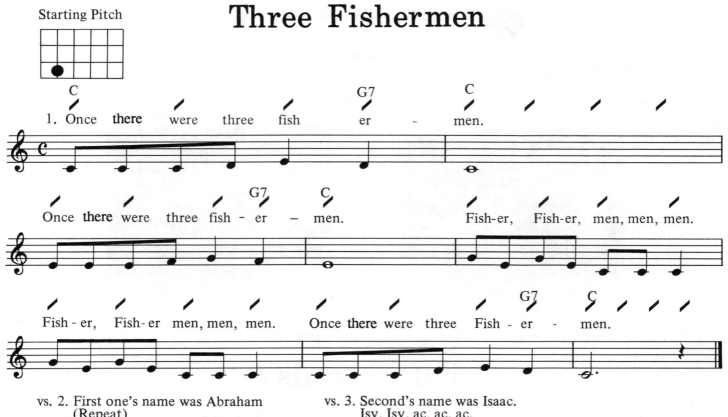

1. Once there were three fish er - men.

Once there were three fish - er - men. Fish-er, Fish-er, men, men, men.

Fish - er, Fish-er men, men, men. Once there were three Fish - er - men.

vs. 2. First one's name was Abraham
(Repeat)
Abra, Abra, ham, ham, ham
(Repeat)
First one's name was Abraham

vs. 3. Second's name was Isaac.
Isy, Isy, ac, ac, ac.

vs. 5. Wish they'd gone to Amsterdam.
Amster, Amster, dam, dam, dam.

vs. 4. Third one's name was Jacob
Jakey, Jakey, cub, cub, cub.

Starting Pitch

Pay Me Money Down

West Indian Folk Song

Chorus Pay me,__ oh, pay me,__ Pay me my mon-ey down,__

Pay me or go to jail,__ Pay me my mon-ey down.__

2. I thought I heard the captain say,
Pay me my money down.
Tomorrow is our sailing day,
Pay me my money down.
Chorus

DOWN-UP STRUM

/ = DOWN STRUM Up till now, we have only been strumming Down Across the strings.

V = UP STRUM   Now we will strum Down and Up.

Down Strum

Up Strum

Try to get a slightly "Swinging" feeling on the Down - Up strum with this song.

Starting Pitch

Buffalo Gals

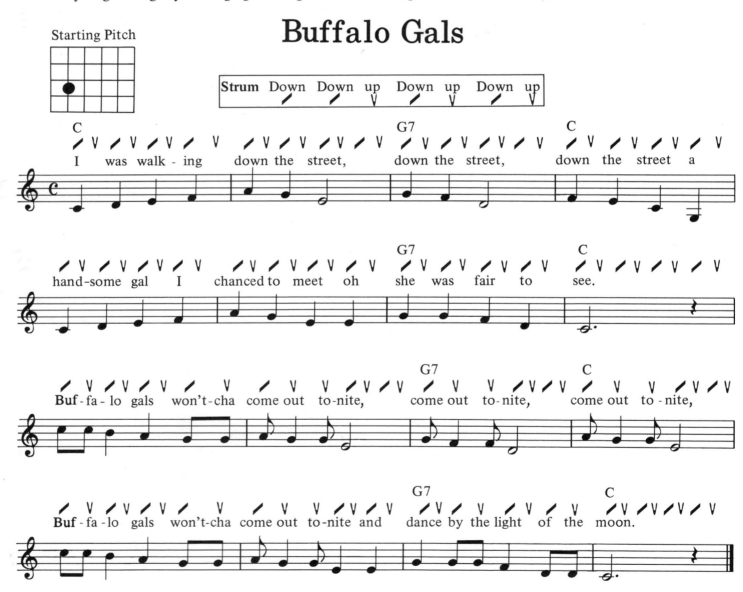

24

He's Got The Whole World

2. He's got the little bitsy baby....   3. He's got you and me brother.....

Hey Lolly

          C
1. Wake up in the mornin', sunny **and** bright
           G7
Hey lolly, lolly lo.
Looked in the mirror, got a terrible fright!
            C
Hey lolly, lolly lo.
   C
2. I have a girl she's ten feet tall,
           G7
Hey lolly, lolly lo.
Sleeps on the floor with her feet in the hall,
         C
Hey lolly, lolly lo.

[make up your own verses]

25

THE "D7" CHORD

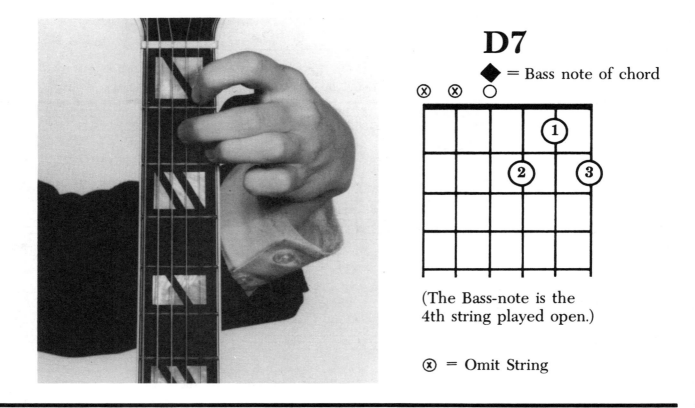

D7

◆ = Bass note of chord

(The Bass-note is the
4th string played open.)

ⓧ = Omit String

Play the following chord study and try to obtain a clear sound with a minimum of movement. Keep the
left hand loose and avoid jerky movements in changing chords.

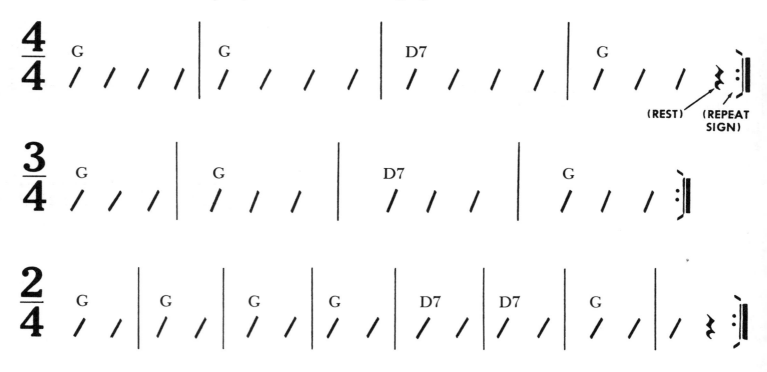

♪ = REST: It indicates a period of silence = to a stroke (/).

Make certain the tone produced is clear. Try to change from the G to D7 chord without looking
at your hands.

Zacchaeus

Children's Gospel Song

Battle Hymn Of The Republic

Starting Pitch

G
1. Mine eyes have seen the glo - ry of the com - ing of the Lord, He is

C **G** **D7**
tramp - ling out the vin - tage where the grapes of wrath are stored, He has

G
loosed the fate - ful light - ning of his ter - ri - ble swift sword, His

C **D7** **G**
truth is march - ing on. Glo - ry, glo - ry, Hal - le -

C **G**
lu - jah! Glo - ry, glo - ry, Hal - le - lu - jah!

C **D7** **G**
Glo - ry, glo - ry, Hal - le - lu - jah! His truth is march - ing on.

            G
2. I have seen Him in the watch fires of a hundred circling camps.
            C   **G**   **D7**
   They have builded Him an altar in the evening dews and damps.
   G
   I have read His righteous sentence by the dim of flaring lamps,
   C   **D7**   **G**
   His truth is marching on.
   G
3. In the beauty of the lilies, Christ was born across the sea,
           C   **G**   **D7**
   With a glory in His bosom that transfigures you and me;
   G
   As He died to make men holy, Let us die to make men free,

       C   **D7**   **G**
   While God is marching on.

28

Hush Little Baby

Children's Song

2. If that billy Goat won't pull,
   mama's Gonna buy you a cart and bull.
   If that cart and bull turn o'er.
   mama's Gonna buy you a dog named rover.

3. If that dog named rover won't bark.
   Mama's gonna buy you a horse and cart.
   If that horse and cart break down,
   You'll still be the sweetest little baby in town.

29

Bile 'Dem Cabbage Down

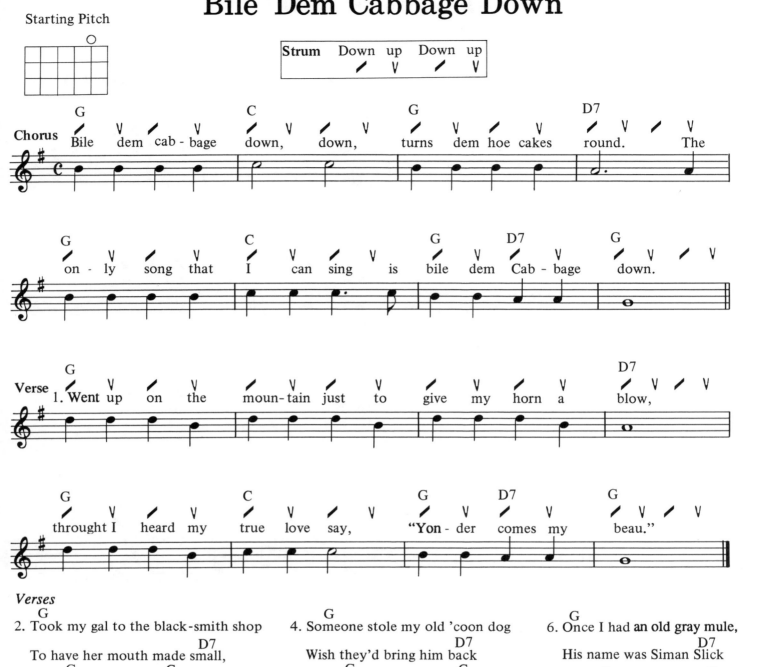

Verses

G
2. Took my gal to the black-smith shop
   D7
   To have her mouth made small,
   G   C
   She turned around a time or two
   G   D7   G
   and swallowed show and all.
   G   *Chorus*
3. Possum in a 'simmon tree,
   G   D7
   Raccoon on the ground,
   Raccoon says, "You son-of-a-gun,
   G   D7   G
   Shake some 'simmons down!"
                    Chorus

                    G
4. Someone stole my old 'coon dog
                    D7
   Wish they'd bring him back
   G   C
   He chased the big hogs thru the fence
            G   D7   G
   And the little ones thru the crack.
   G   *Chorus*
5. Met a possum in the road
                    D7
   Blind as he could be,
   G   C
   Jumped the fence and whipped my dog.
   And bristled up at me.
                    Chorus

                    G
6. Once I had **an old gray mule**,
                    D7
   His name was Siman Slick
            G   C
   He'd roll his eyes and back his ear
            G   D7   G
   And how that mule would kick!
   G   *Chorus*
7. I've heard some folks tell **a tale**
                    D7
   There's gold in them thar hills,
            G   C
   But I lived up there forty years
            G   D7   G
   And all I seen was stills!
                    Chorus

Away In A Manger

This Little Light Of Mine

31

HOLDING THE PICK

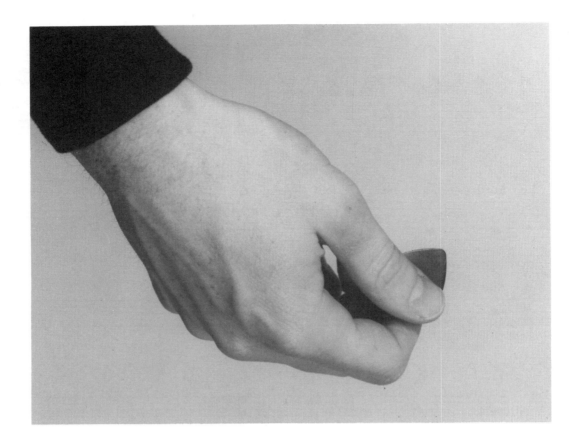

Now is the time to introduce the use of the flat pick. Study the photograph carefully, make certain that the pick is not held too tightly. Practice strumming up and down with the flat pick in order to get the feel of it. (The student may continue to use his thumb at this point if so desired by the teacher.) Make careful note of the symbols used to denote down pick and up pick. This will be used throughout as we learn to pick notes.

Check your hand position. Do not hold the pick too tight!

/ = Down Strum   ∨ = Up Strum

Peace Like A River

Starting Pitch

Strum	Down	Down	Down	up	Down	up

G   C

1. I've got peace like a riv-er, I've got peace like a riv-er, I've got

G   D7   G

peace like a riv-er in my soul; I've got peace like a riv-er I've got

C   G   D7   G

peace like a riv-er, I've got peace like a riv-er in my soul.

2. I've got joy like a fountain   3. I've got love like an **ocean**.

All Through The Night

Starting Pitch

Slowly

Strum	Down	Down	Down	up

G   C   D7   C   D7   G

Sleep, my child, and peace at-tend thee. All through the night.
Guar-dian an-gels, God will send thee all through the night. *(Repeat)*

C   D7

Soft and drow-sy hours are creep-ing, hill and vale in slum-ber sleep-ing

G   C   D7   C   D7   G

I am lov-ing vig-il keep-ing all through the night.

2.
     G   C   D7   C D7   G

While the moon her watch is keeping, all through the night.
     G   C D7   C D7   G

While the weary world is sleeping, all through the night.
     C

O'er thy spirit gently stealing,
          D7

Visions of delight revealing,
     G   C   D7   C D7   G

Breathes a pure and holy feeling, all through the night.

Blow, Ye Winds

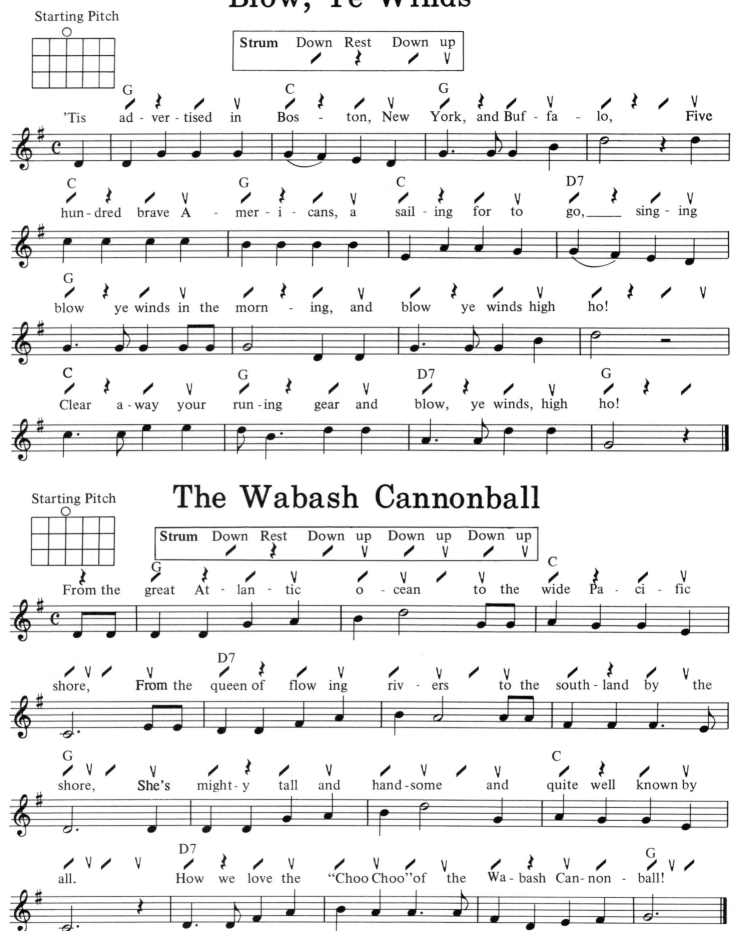

The Wabash Cannonball

Down By The Riverside

2. I'm gonna join hands with everyone, etc.
3. I'm gonna put on my long white robe, etc.
4. I'm gonna talk with the **Prince of Peace,** etc.

Go Tell It On The Mountain

Starting Pitch

Strum	Down	up	Down	up	Down	Down
	/	V	/	V	/	/

G
/ V / V / / V / V /
Go   tell it on the moun - tain,   ov - er the hill and

G / V / V /   **D7** / V / V /   **G** / V / V /
ev' - ry - where,___   go   tell it on the moun - tain that

/ V / V /   **D7** / V / V /   **G** V / V /
Je - sus   Christ___ is   **born!**   Oh,   when   I   was   a

/ V / V / /   **D7** / V / V /   **G** / V / V / /
sin - ner,   I   prayed both night and   day,   I   asked the Lord to

/ V / V /   **C** / V / V /   **D7** / V / V /
help   me,   and   He   showed   me   the   way._____

Full G7 Chord

G7

Practice Study

G	G7	C	D7	G	D7	G

She'll Be Coming Round The Mountain

The Gospel Train

2. The fare is cheap and all can go,
The rich and poor are there;
No second class aboard this train,
No difference in the fare. Chorus

3. I hear that train a-comin',
She sure is speedin' fast,
So get your tickets ready
And ride to heaven at last. Chorus

THE KEY OF D

The three basic chords in the key of D are: D, G, and A7.

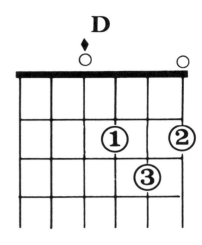

D

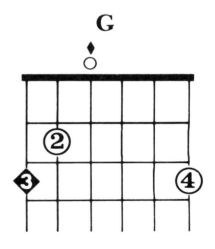

G

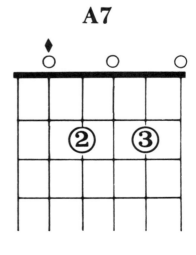

A7

O = Open Strings
♦ = Bass Note of Chord

Old Joe Clark

2. Old Joe Clark, the preacher's son,
   Preached all over the plain,
   The only text he ever knew
       C   D
   Was "high, low jack and the game."
   D   *Chorus*
3. Old Joe Clark had a mule,
   His name was Morgan Brown,
   'And every tooth in that mule's head
       C   D
   Was sixteen inches around.
                   Chorus

4. Old Joe Clark had a house
   Fifteen stories high
   And every story in that house
       C   D
   Was filled with chicken pie.
   D   *Chorus*
5. I went down to old Joe's house
   He invited me to supper,
   I stumped my toe on the table leg
            C   D
   And stuck my nose in the butter.
                   Chorus

She Wore a Yellow Ribbon

American
Folk Song

D

But, in her heart, she has a secret passion

A7

She has it in the springtime, and in the month of May;

D

And if you asked her who is now her passion,

A7   D

She has it for a college man who's not so far away.

Chorus

Give Me Oil in My Lamp

2. Give me joy in my heart, keep me singing,
3. Place your peace in my soul, keep me sharing,
4. Place your faith in my heart, keep me trusting,

When The Saints Go Marchin' In

2. And when they gather 'round the throne.
3. And when they crown him **King** of kings
4. And on that Hallelujah day.

Streets Of Laredo

Starting Pitch

Strum Down Down up Down Down Down Down

D

As I _____ walked out in the streets of La - re - do, as

D

I walked out in La - re - do one day, I

D

spied a young cow - boy wrapped up in white lin - en, wrapped

D

up in white lin - en as cold as the clay.

D   A7   D   A7
2. "Go fetch me a cup, a cup of cold water,
D   A7   D   A7
To cool my parched lips," the cowboy then said;
D   A7   D   A7
Before I returned, the spirit had left him
D   G   A7   D
And gone to its Maker - the cowboy was dead.

D   A7   D   A7
3. We beat the drum slowly and played the fife lowly,
D   A7   D   A7
And bitterly wept as we bore him along;
D   A7   D   A7
For we all loved our comrade, so brave, young, and handsome,
D   G   A7   D
We all loved our comrade although he'd done wrong.

Crawdad Song

Starting Pitch

Strum Down Rest Down up

D

You get a line and I'll get a pole, Hon - ey, Hon - ey,

You get a line and I'll get a pole, Babe, ___ Babe, ___

D   D7   G

You get a line and I'll get a pole, We'll go down to the

D   A7   D   G   D

craw - dad hole, Hon - ey, sug - ar ba - by mine. _____

Oh! Susanna

The Girl I Left Behind Me

Starting Pitch

Strum Down Rest Down up

I am lone-some since I crossed the hill and o'er the moor and val - ley, such a
heav - y throught my heart do fill since part - ing with my__ Las - sie. I__
seek no more the joy in life, for ech - oes but re - mind me how__
swift the hours did pass a - way with the girl I left be - hind me.

Li'l Liza Jane

Starting Pitch

Strum Down Rest Down up Down up Down up

I got a gal and you got none Li'l Liz - a Jane,
I got a gal that calls me hon; Li'l Liz - a Jane.

Chorus Oh E - liz - a, Li'l Liz - a Jane,
Oh E - liz - a, Li'l Liz - a Jane.

Frankie & Johnny

Come And Go With Me

2. There'll be singin' in that land
3. There'll be dancin' in that land.
4. There is freedom in that land
5. There is love in that land.

THE KEY OF A

The three basic chords in the key of A are: A, D, and E7.

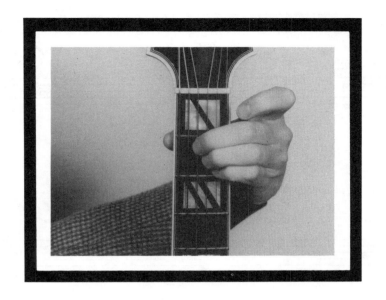

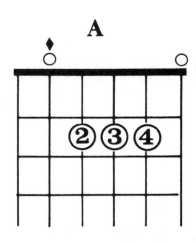

A

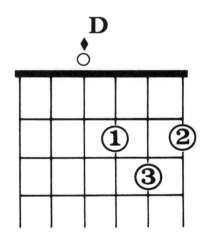

D

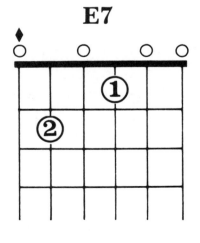

E7

O = Open Strings
♦ = Bass Note of Chord

Just A Closer Walk

2. I am weak and thou art strong;
   Jesus keep me from all wrong;
   I'll be satisfied as long
   As I walk, let me walk close to thee.

3. Through this world of **toil and snares,**
   If I **falter,** Lord, who cares?"
   Guide me gently, safely o'er
   To Thy kingdom shore, to Thy shore.

4. Repeat Vs. 1

Hand Me Down My Walking Cane

Starting Pitch

Rock Of Ages

Starting Pitch

49

Worried Man Blues

Starting Pitch

Syncopated Strum Down Down up hold up Down up
hold

A
It takes a wor-ried man to sing a wor-ried song. It

D
takes a wor-ried man to sing a wor-ried song, It

takes a wor-ried man to sing a wor-ried song, I'm wor-ried

E7
now, But I won't be wor-ried long.

1. I went across the river, I lay down to sleep,
   When I woke up, had shackles on my feet.
   Chorus

2. I asked that judge, tell me, what's gonna be my fine?
   Twenty-one years on the Rocky Mountain Line.
   Chorus

3. Twenty-one years to pay my awful crime,
   Twenty-one years-but I got ninety-nine.
   Chorus

Green Grow The Lilacs

Starting Pitch

Strum Down up Down Down

A
Green grow the li-lacs all spark-ling with dew, I'm

E7
lone-ly, my dar-ling, since part-ing with you. But

A   A7   D
by our next meet-ing I'll hope to prove true, and

E7   A   E7   A
change the green li-lacs to the Red, White, and blue.

Little Brown Jug

Old Dan Tucker

Old Time Religion

2. It was good for my father   3. It was good for the Hebrew children.

Do, Lord

THE KEY OF E MINOR

The three basic chords in the key of E minor are: Em, Am, and B7.

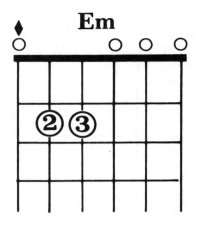
Em

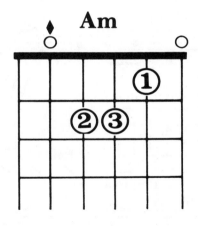
Am

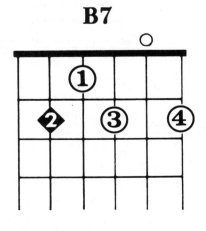
B7

O = Open Strings
♦ = Bass Note of Chord

53

Wade In The Water

Wayfarin' Stranger

What Child Is This?

The God Of Abraham Praise

Oh God, We Praise Thee

56

Oh, Sinner Man

What Shall We Do With The Drunken Sailor?

CHORUS   Hooray, and up she rises, (3 times)
         Earlye in the morning.

2. Throw 'im in the Brig until he rises (3 times)
   Earlye in the morning. (Chrous)

3. Send 'im a climbin' up to the crows nest (3 times)
   Earlye in the morning. (Chorus)

Joshua Fit The Battle Of Jericho

I Will Arise And Go To Jesus

Southern Folk Hymn

THE KEY OF C

The three basic chords in the key of C are: C, F, and G7.

C

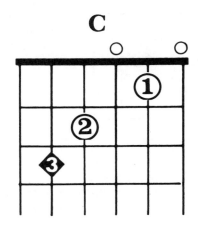

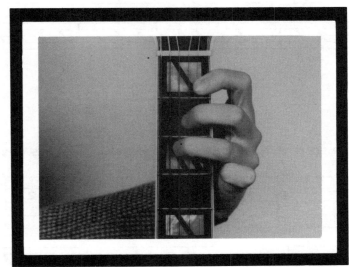

F

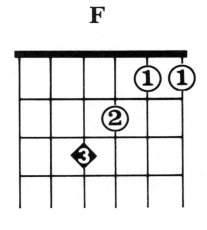

G7

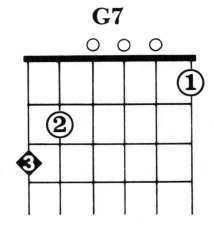

O = Open Strings
♦ = Bass Note of Chord

59

The F Chord

(Student plays the top 4 strings)

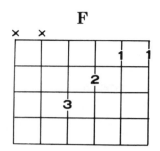

F

To play the F chord - make sure your left hand thumb is on the center of the back of the neck. If you wrap your thumb around the neck so that it touches the 6th string, you will have problems fingering the F chord.

Building the F chord

Play the following exercise until the tone sounds clear. You will start on the 1st fret and end on the 7th fret.

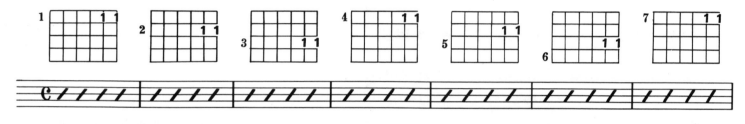

Now play this exercise from the 1st to the 7th fret until it sounds clear.

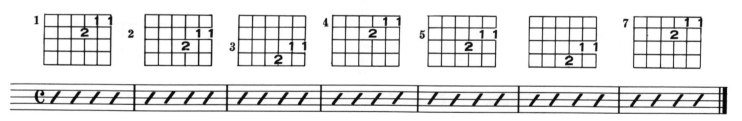

Play from 1st to 7th fret until it sounds clear.

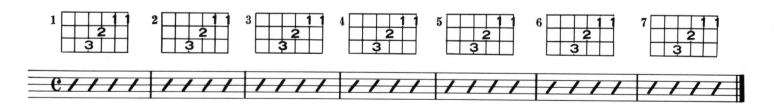

On Top Of Old Smoky

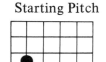

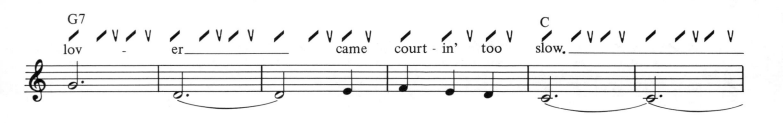

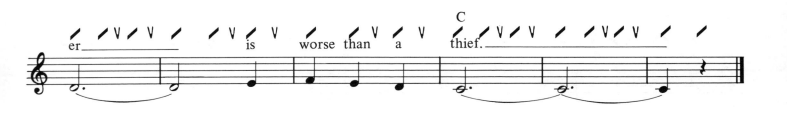

There Is A Tavern In The Town

62

The Marine's Hymn

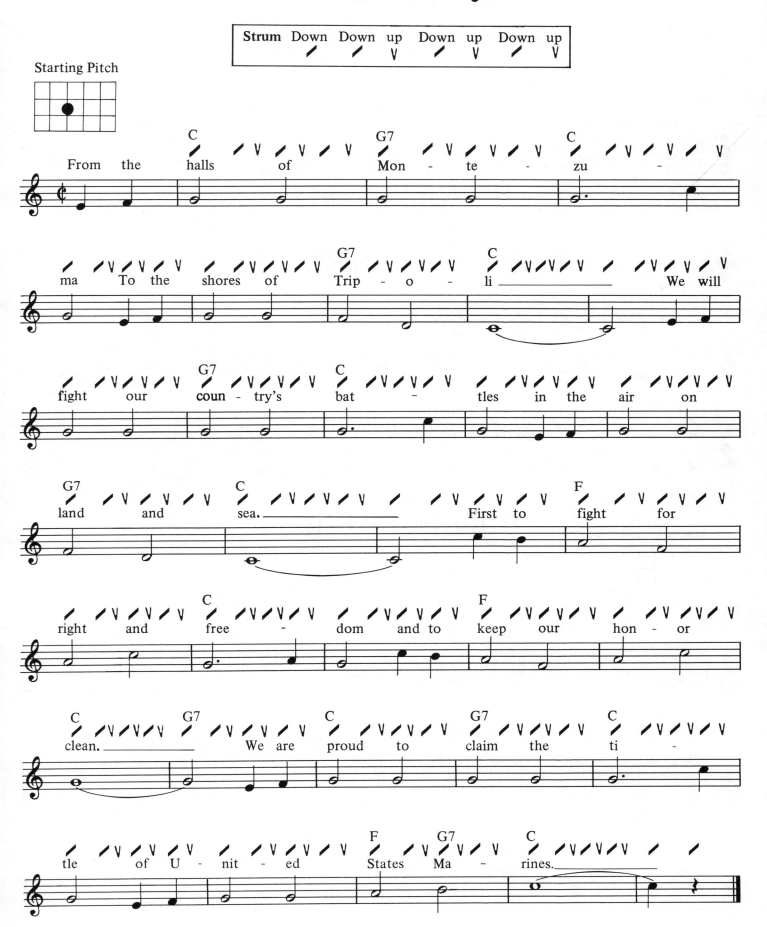

Camptown Races

Railroad Bill

Every Time I Feel The Spirit

Standing In The Need Of Prayer

Wildwood Flower

Our Boys Will Shine Tonight

Yellow Rose Of Texas

Strum	Down	up	Down	Down	up	Down	up

There's a yel-low rose in Tex-as I'm go-in' for to see, no

oth-er fel-low knows her; no-bod-y else but me. She

cried so when I left her it like to broke my heart, and

if I ev-er find her, we nev-er more will part.

Swanee River

Strum	Down	Down	up	Down	Down

'Way down up on the Swa-nee riv-er, far, far a-way.

There's where my heart is turn-ing ev-er, there's where the old folks stay.

THE KEY OF E

The three basic chords in the key of E are: E, A, and B7.

E

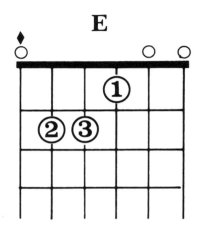

A

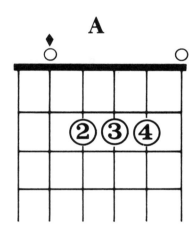

B7

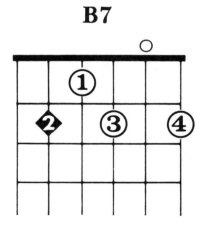

O = Open Strings
♦ = Bass Note of Chord

Swing Low, Sweet Chariot

2. When I get to glory, my voice I'll raise,
   (E   A   E)
Comin' for to carry me home,
   (B7)
To sing a song of grateful praise,
   (A E A   E)
Comin' for to carry me home.
   (B7   E)

Sweet By and By

2. We shall sing on that beautiful shore
They melodious songs of blest;
And our spirits shall sorrow no more
Not a sigh for the blessing of rest.

3. To our bountiful Father above
We will offer our tribute of praise,
For the glorious gift of His love
And the blessings that hallow our days.

70

Beautiful Brown Eyes

Goin' Down The Road Feelin' Bad

This Train

Mary Ann

Basic Blues Rhythm

Of-ten **when** I **pass** this **way**

I **feel** as **though** I **ought** to **stay**

But **life** keeps **driv**-in' **me** a-**way**

un-**til** a-**noth**-er **rain**-y **day**.

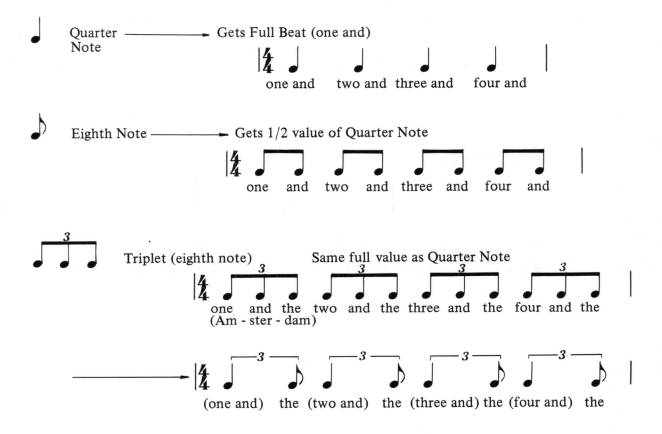

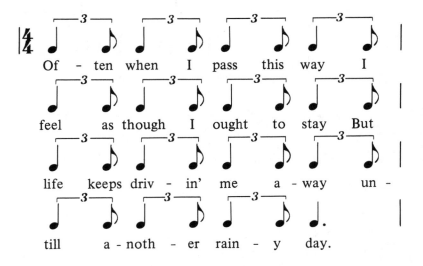

Blues Shuffle Rhythm

Slidin' Into E

Try the above Shuffle Rhythm with the following Lick:

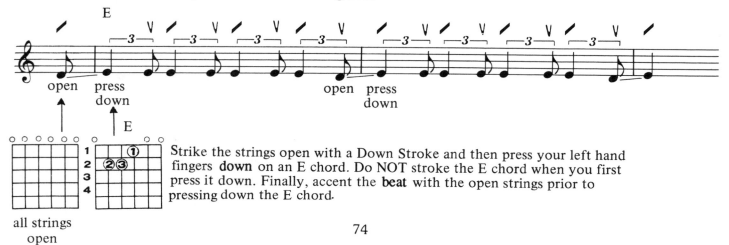

Strike the strings open with a Down Stroke and then press your left hand fingers **down** on an E chord. Do NOT stroke the E chord when you first press it down. Finally, accent the **beat** with the open strings prior to pressing down the E chord.

74

12th Street and Delmar

[2nd String Open = Starting Pitch]

Chords E - A - B7

Slow groove

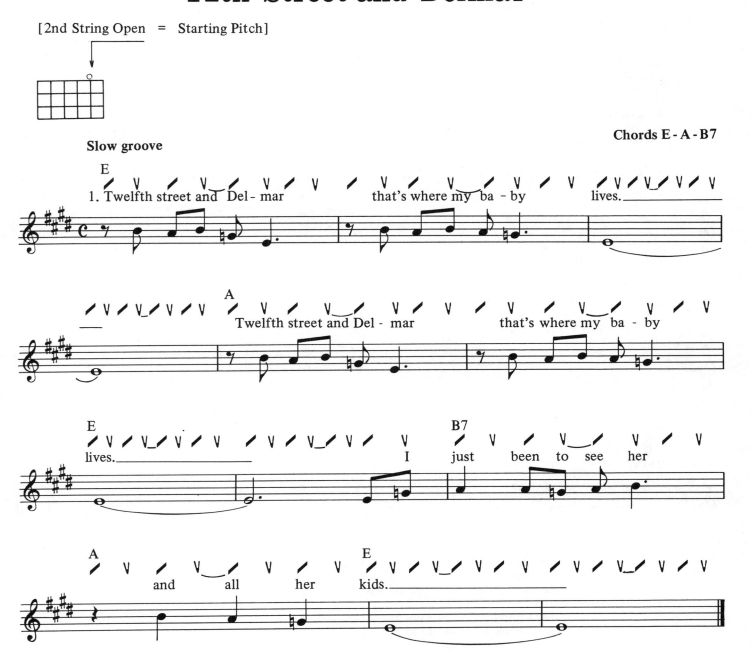

2. Twelfth street and Delmar, you're crowdin' me.
   Twelfth street and Delmar, you're crowdin' me.
   You didn't think that I would
   Begin to see.

3. Twelfth street and Delmar, I ain't gonna stay.
   Twelfth street and Delmar, I ain't gonna stay.
   You want to marry me,
   There ain't no way.

Down and Out

[4th String, 2nd Fret = Starting Pitch]

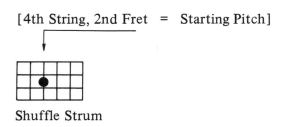

Shuffle Strum

Slow groove

Chords: E - A - B7

1. Tired and wear - y I got___ the blues. _____

A
Tried and wear - y I got___ the Blues. E _____

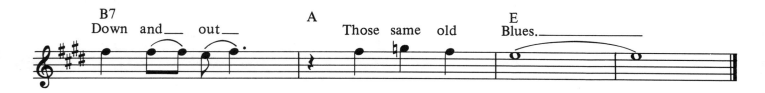

B7
Down and___ out___ A Those same old E Blues._____

2. Boss just fired me - More bad news
   Boss just fired me - More bad news
   He didn't want me - Those same old Blues.

3. (My) Baby left me - I got the Blues.
   (My) Baby left me - I got the Blues
   She up and left me - More down out Blues.

4. Down and out - I got the Blues.
   Down and out - I got the Blues.
   No ambition - Those same old Blues.

"BLUE NOTES"

The circled notes below are notes that can be added to the chords to give them a more varied blues effect.

Basic Chord

Blue Notes Circled

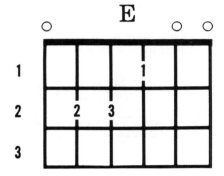

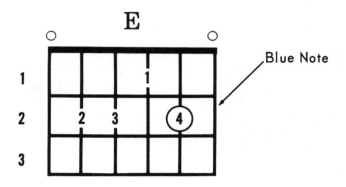

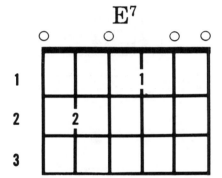

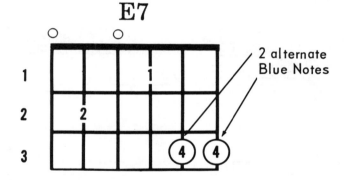

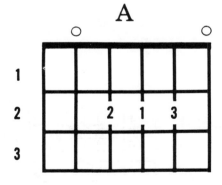

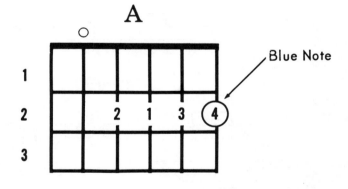

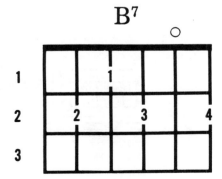

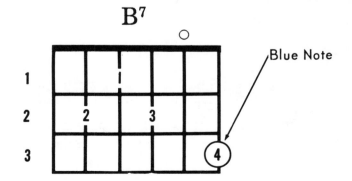

Blue Note Exercise

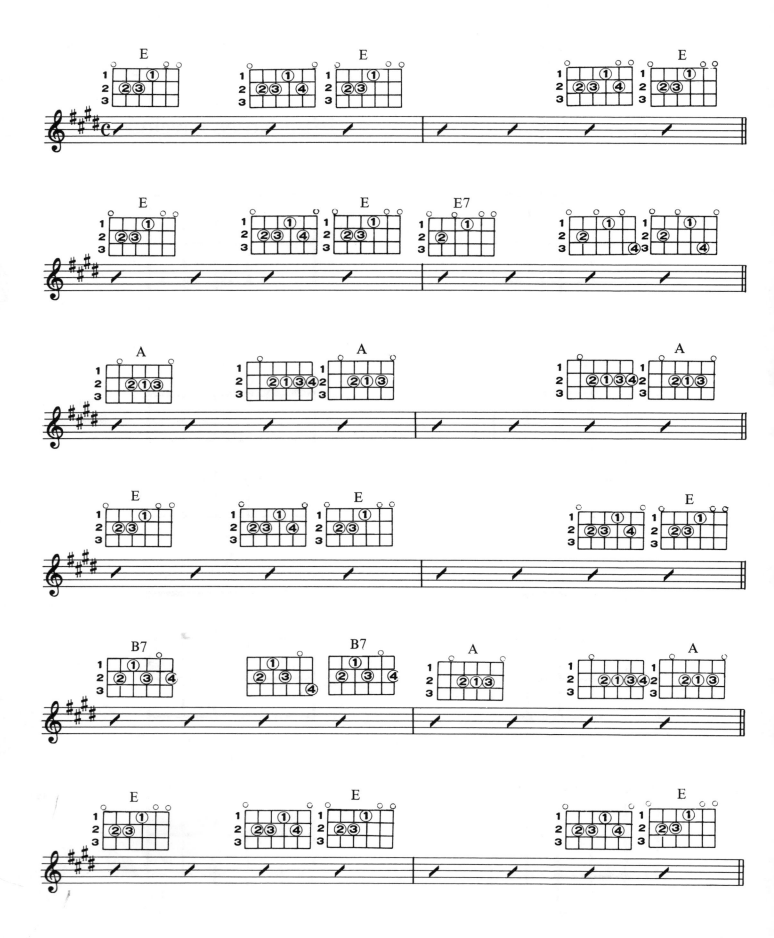

City Slicker

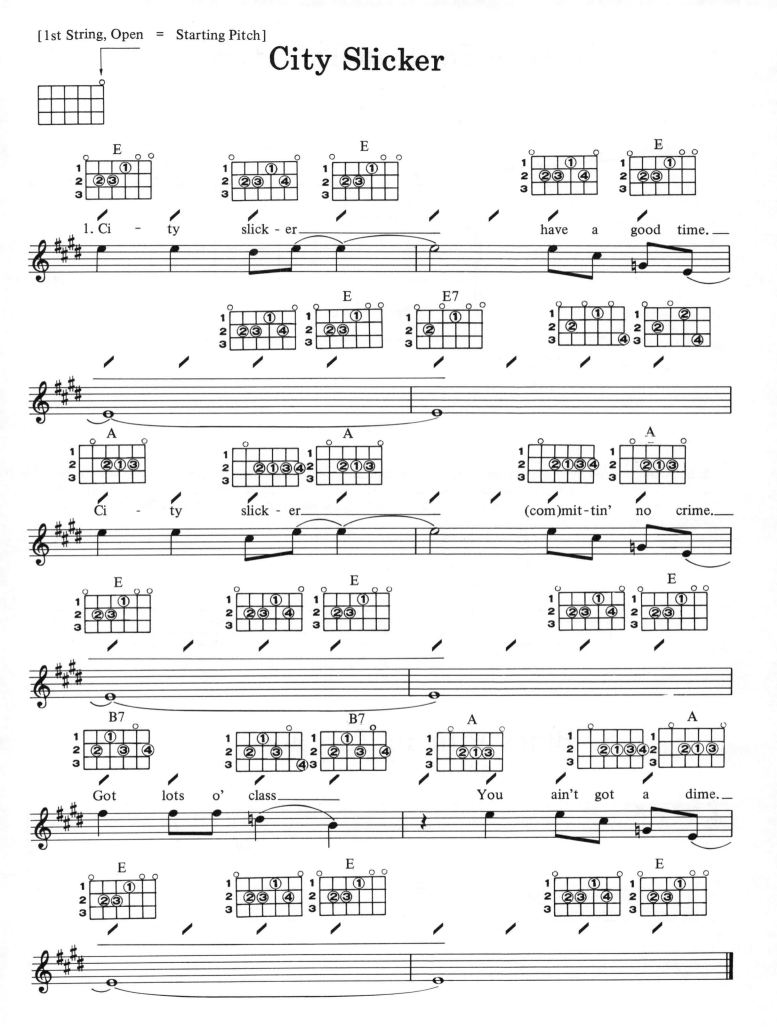

How To Read Tablature

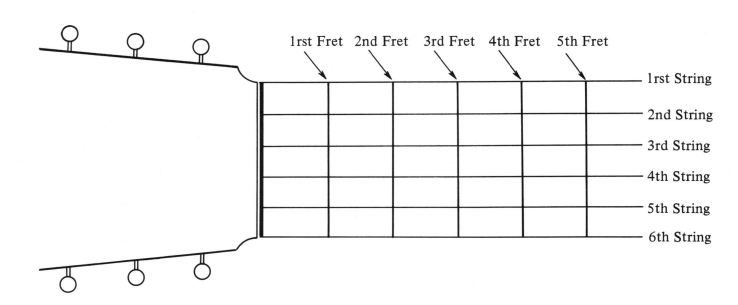

In tablature the lines represent strings. The numbers appearing on the lines indicate frets (0 = open string). In the following example a C chord would be played. (1st string open; 2nd string press down on the 1st fret; 3rd string open; 4th string press down on the 2nd fret; 5th string press down on the 3rd fret; and, finally, do not play the 6th string.)

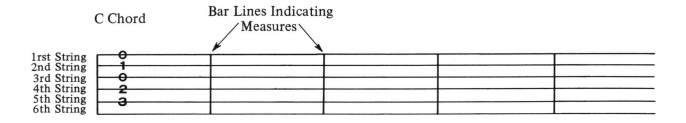

Blues Run In Tab Form

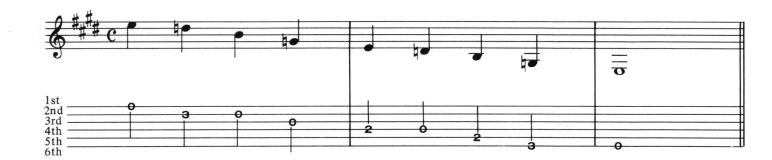

80

Blues Endings
(Phrases or "Licks" Starting on Measure 11 of 12 Bar Blues)

Single Note Finger Style Lick

With this Ending Lick the player will play three triplets, plucking the notes with the Right Hand. The Fingering would be:

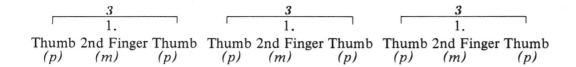

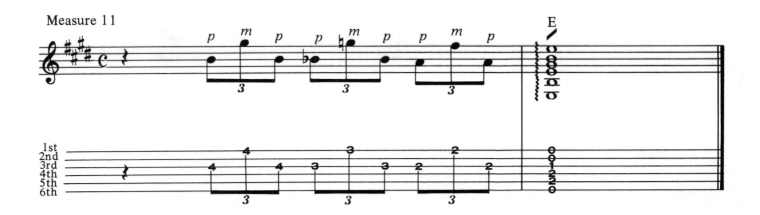

Chromatic Slide Ending

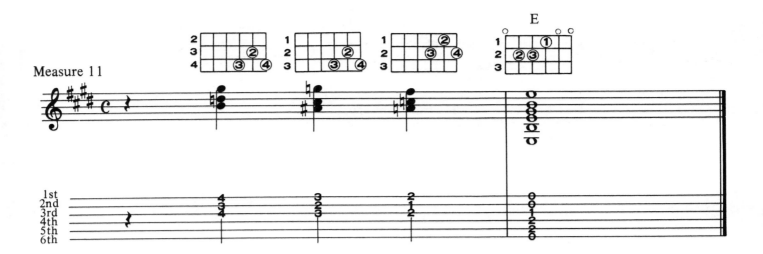

Pushin and A Pullin'

[4th String, 2nd Fret = Starting Pitch]

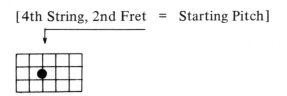

Moderate

E

1. Push-in' and a pull-in'   Bid in' my time.___   Push-in' and a pull-in'

E7   A

ev - ry   day   I'm   out   shove-lin' co - al___   Hurts   my back___ I'm just

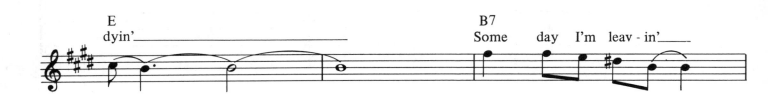

E   B7

dyin'_____   Some   day   I'm   leav - in'___

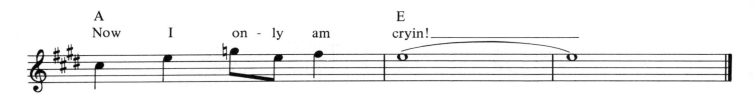

A   E

Now   I   on - ly   am   cryin!_____

2. Fifty cents an hour - earnin' my pay.
   Pushin' and a pullin' - every day I'm
   Out lookin' elsewhere - ain't no jobs for my kind.
   Someday I'm leavin' - now get back to the grind.

Shuffle Rhythm

The Shuffle Rhythm was popularized by many of the early Rock Musicians. It adds a Boogie - Woogie type of feeling to the Blues.

Blues Shuffle Boogie

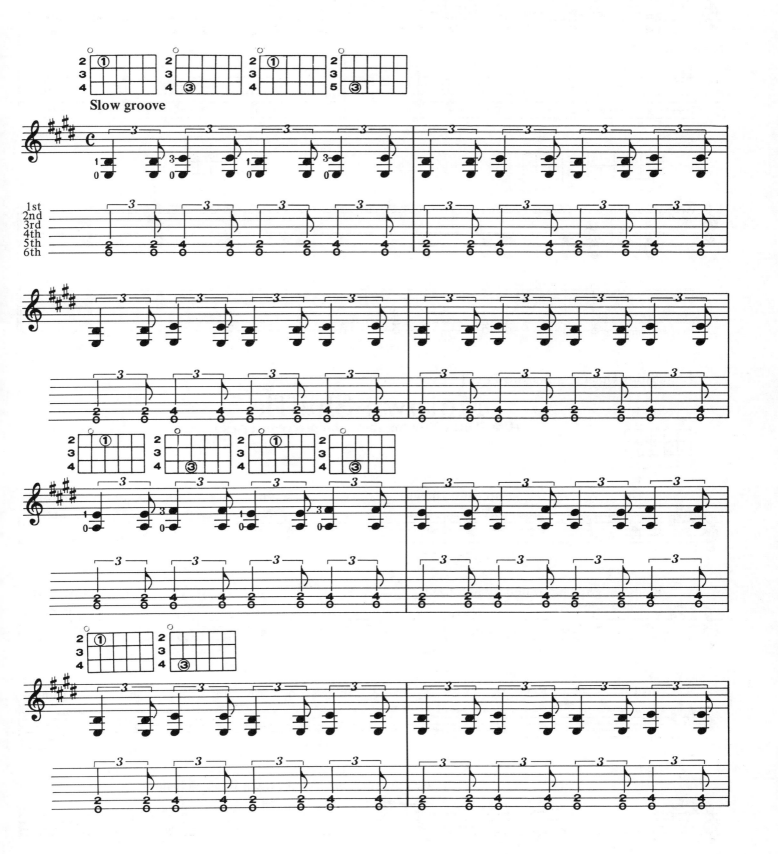

[2nd String Open = Starting Pitch]

Motown Shuffle
(Use Shuffle Rhythm shown on preceeding page)

E
1. Up   up and down   in and out   up and down Mo-town

Blues go-in' round my head.___   ain't dead___   But I

E
feel like I'm dy-in' 'cause there's no use in try-in' a-gain.___

B7   A   E   B7
___ mm _____   Got them old Mo-town Blues a-gain._____

84

The Bend (‿)

The Bend is a great Blues effect. It is achieved by
pushing a string towards the next largest string.
This alters the pitch of that particular note.

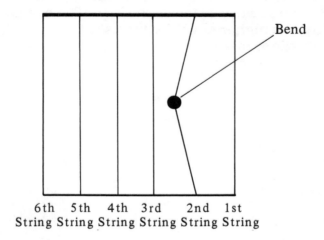

6th   5th   4th   3rd   2nd   1st
String String String String String String

Blues Run

Try this on the E Chord.
Also try Bending various
notes in the Run.

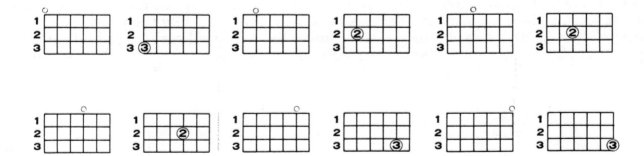

Once you have gained fluency in playing this Run going up, try playing it coming down.

THE CAPO
(pronounced kay-pō)

Frequently a singer may want to sing a song in a different key from the one you know. In order to meet this demand you will have to raise or lower the key. The easiest way to raise the pitch of the instrument and thereby play in a higher key is by the use of a capo. Capos can be purchased at any music store and are either elastic or metal. While the metal capo is stronger, the elastic one is often less likely to scratch the neck of your guitar.

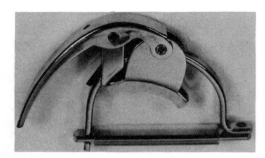

Metal Capo

Elastic Capo

HOW TO USE THE CAPO

The key you are playing in is raised ½ step each time you move the capo up one fret. As an example, play your E chord. Next place the capo on the first fret, move your hand up one fret, finger and play your E chord. It sounds higher, doesn't it! The most practical way of raising the pitch or key is by the use of barre chords. With barre chords your first finger lies across all six strings and serves as your capo. Capos enable the player to obtain the ringing sound of open strings in all keys. This is very useful to the folk and bluegrass performer.

THE KEY OF A MINOR

The basic chords in the key of A minor are: Am, Dm, and E7.

Am

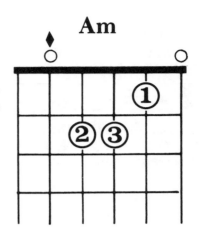

Dm

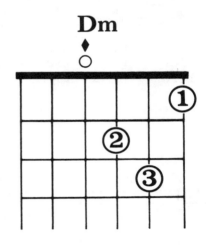

E7

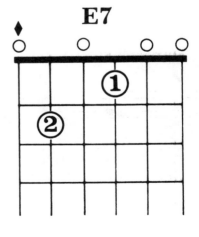

O = Open Strings
♦ = Bass Note of Chord

87

Coventry Carol

Starting Pitch

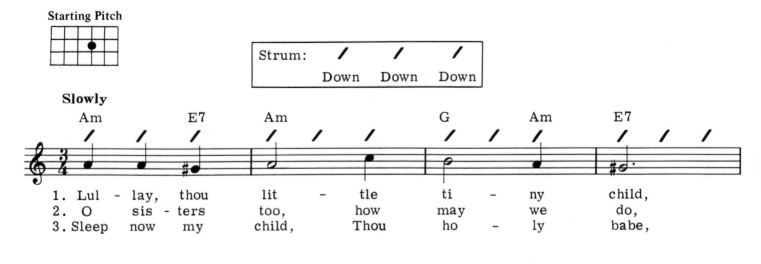

Strum: / / /
Down Down Down

Slowly

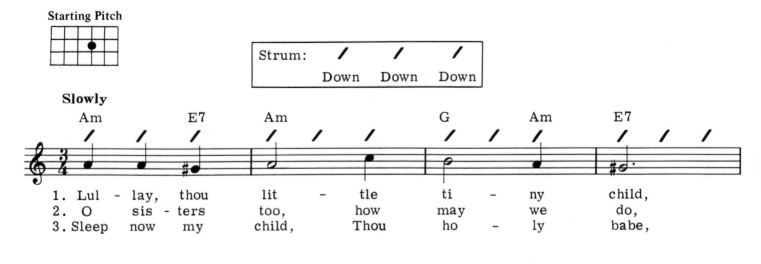

1. Lul - lay, thou lit - tle ti - ny child,
2. O sis - ters too, how may we do,
3. Sleep now my child, Thou ho - ly babe,

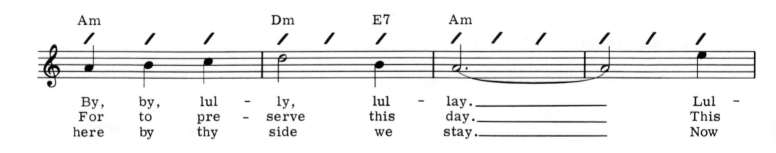

By, by, lul - ly, lul - lay._____ Lul -
For to pre - serve this day._____ This
here by thy side we stay._____ Now

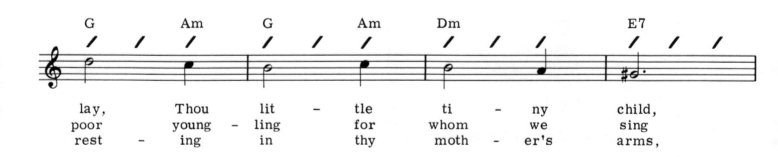

lay, Thou lit - tle ti - ny child,
poor young - ling for whom we sing
rest - ing in thy moth - er's arms,

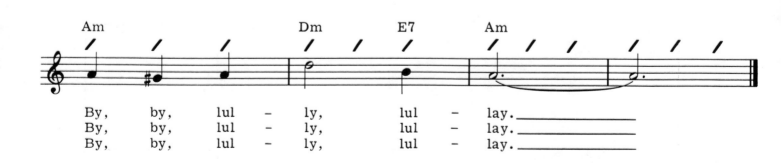

By, by, lul - ly, lul - lay._____
By, by, lul - ly, lul - lay._____
By, by, lul - ly, lul - lay._____

When Johnny Comes Marching Home

MASTER CHORD

MAJOR KEY

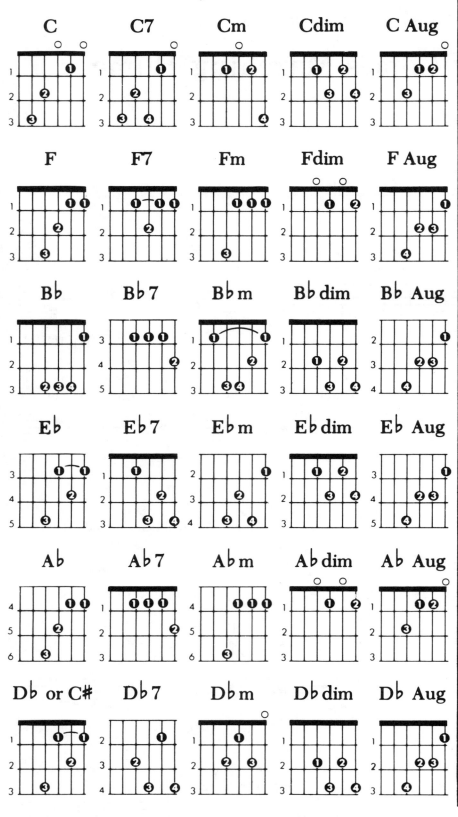

RELATIVE MINOR

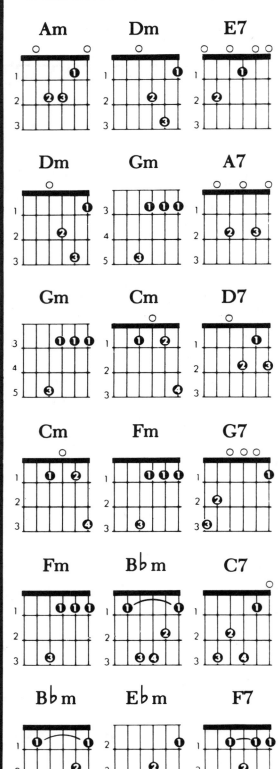

REFERENCE CHART

MAJOR KEY

RELATIVE MINOR

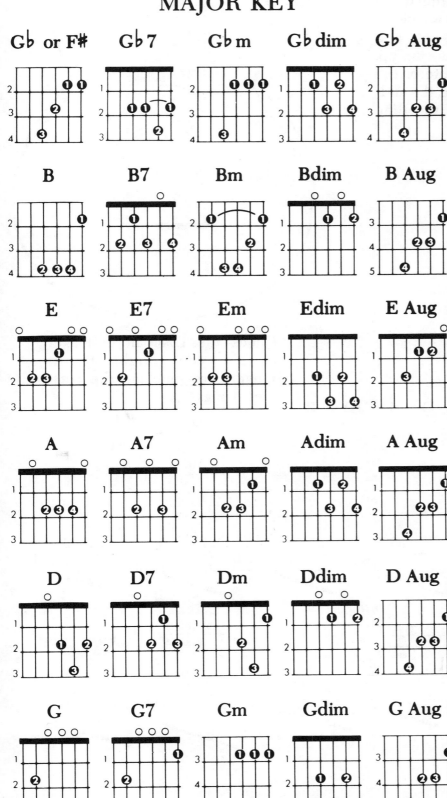

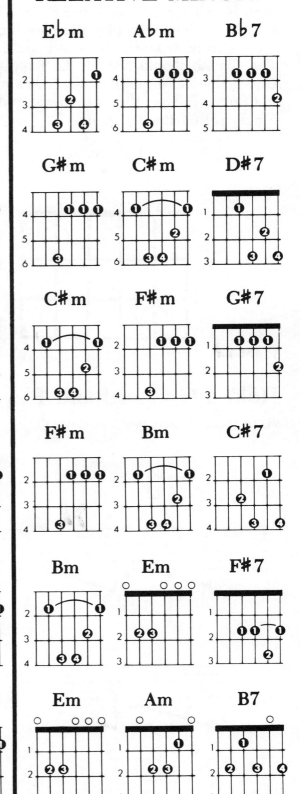

ARPEGGIO PICKING
(BROKEN CHORDS)

Arpeggio style playing is especially beautiful when used as an accompaniment to a Ballad. Basically all the player does is to play the chord, a note at a time, starting from the bass note and moving up. The Thumb should rest on the Bass note of the Chord, the 1st Finger (i) on the 3rd string, the middle finger (m) on the 2nd string, and the Ring Finger (a) on the 1st string.

Left Hand

C

Right Hand   p   i   m   a

Check the Diagram to make certain your Right Hand Fingers are plucking the correct strings.

Hold a C Chord and Play: p - i - m - a
Arpeggio Exercise:

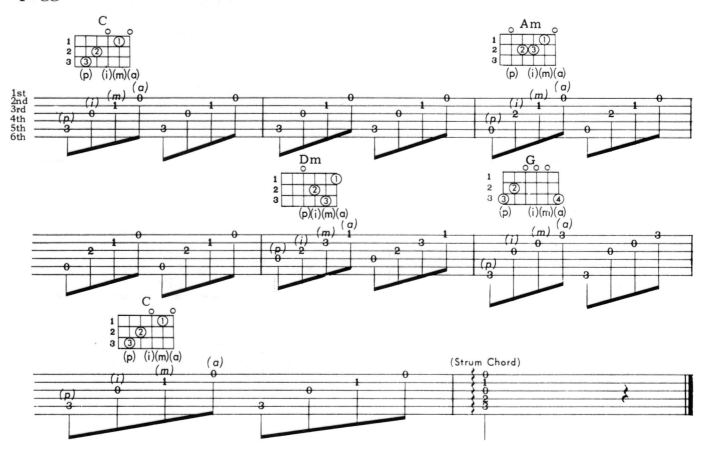

Kum Ba Yah

African Spiritual

[5th String, 3rd Fret = Starting Pitch]

Moderately

1. Kum-ba - ya, my Lord, _____ Kum-ba ya, _____ Kum-ba -
ya, my Lord _____ Kum-ba - ya, _____ Kum-ba -
ya, my Lord, _____ Kum-ba - ya, _____ Oh,
Lord, _____ Kum-ba - ya.

2. Someone's singing, Lord, Kumbaya   3. Someone's weeping, Lord, Kumbaya
4. Someone's praying, Lord, Kumbaya

Shenandoah

[6th String, 3rd Fret = Strting Pitch]

Slowly

Mel.

1. Oh, Shen-an-doah,___ I long to hear you, A - way,___ you roll-ing

Acc.

riv - er.___ Oh Shen-an-doah ___ I long to hear you, A -

way,___ we're bound a - way, 'Cross the wide Mis - sou - ri.

2. The white man loved the Indian maiden,
Away, you rolling river
With notions his canoe was laden,
Away, we're bound away,
'Cross the wide Missouri.

3. O, Shenandoah, I love your daughter,
Away, you rolling river
I'll take her 'cross the rolling water,
Away, we're bound away,
'Cross the wide Missouri.

4. O, Shenandoah, I'm bound to leave you,
Away, you rolling river,
O, Shenandoah, I'll not deceive you,
Away, we're bound away,
'Cross the wide Missouri.

94

My Faith Looks Up to Thee

Balm in Gilead

Were You There?

ALTERNATE BASS

An interesting variation on the standard arpeggio picking is the use of alternate basses. With alternate basses the guitarist plays his arpeggio as usual; however, he plucks an alternate bass note with his thumb the second time that the arpeggio is played.

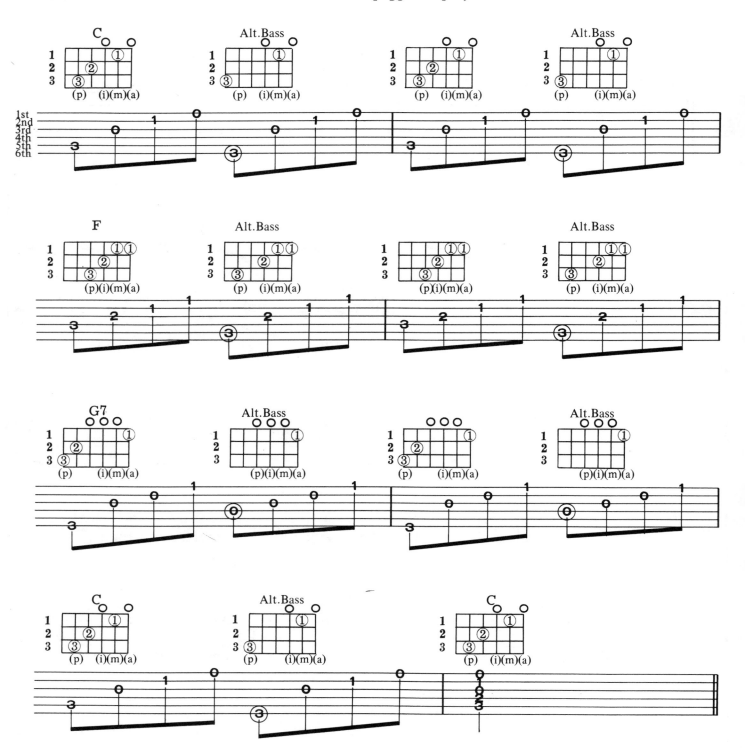

ALTERNATE G7 CHORD

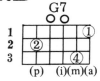

This form of the G7 chord lends itself exceptionally well to finger style playing. Try substituting it into songs in place of the standard G7 fingering.

Long, Long Ago

(Using Alternate Basses)

[5th String—3rd Fret = Starting Pitch]

On Jordan's Stormy Banks

Samuel Stennett
1727-1795

American Folk Melody

Starting Pitch

Lively tempo

1. On Jor-dan's storm-y banks I stand, And cast a wish-ful eye To
2. O'er all those wide ex-tend-ed plains Shines one e-ter-nal day; There
3. When I shall reach that hap-py place, I'll be for-ev-er blest, For

Ca-naan's fair and hap-py land, Where my pos-ses-sions lie, O___
God the Son for-ev-er-reigns, And scat-ters night a-way. No___
I shall see my Fa-ther's face, And in his bos-om rest. Filled

the trans-port-ing rap-turous scene That ris-ses to my sight: Sweet
chill-ing winds of poi-sonous breath Can reach that health-ful shore; Sick-
with de-light my rap-tured soul Lives out its earth-ly day; And

fields ar-rayed in liv-ing green And riv-ers of de-light!
ness and sor-row, pain and death, Are falt and feared no more.
then, though Jor-dan's waves may roll, I'll fear-less launch a-way.

100

3/4 Arpeggio Strum

You will remember that in $\frac{3}{4}$ time you count 1-2-3, 1-2-3, etc. The arpeggio pattern in $\frac{3}{4}$ time is most commonly p-i-m-a-m-a. You simply play the standard arpeggio (p-i-m-a) and repeat the last 2 notes (m-a).

Exercise 1

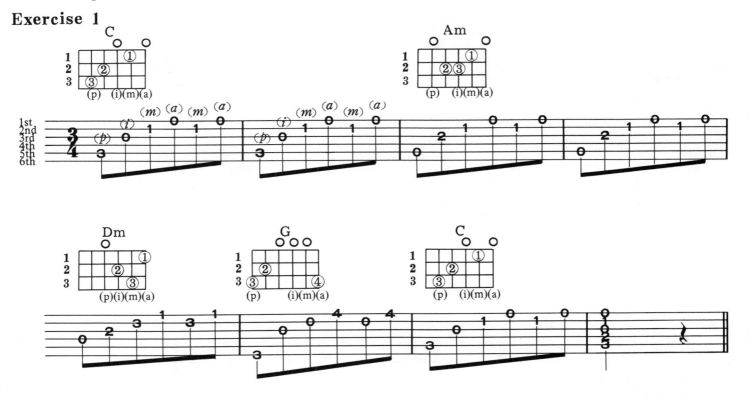

Exercise 2

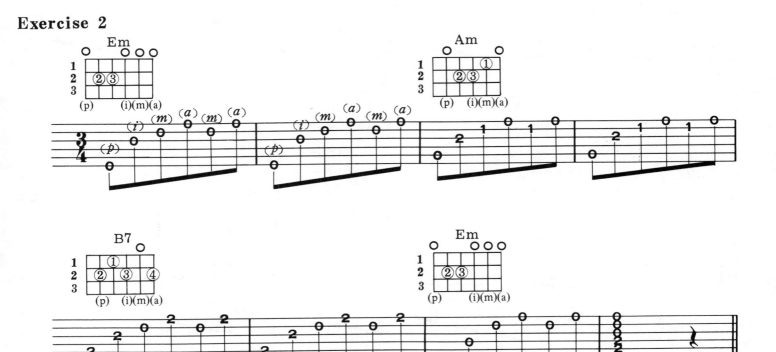

101

Down in the Valley

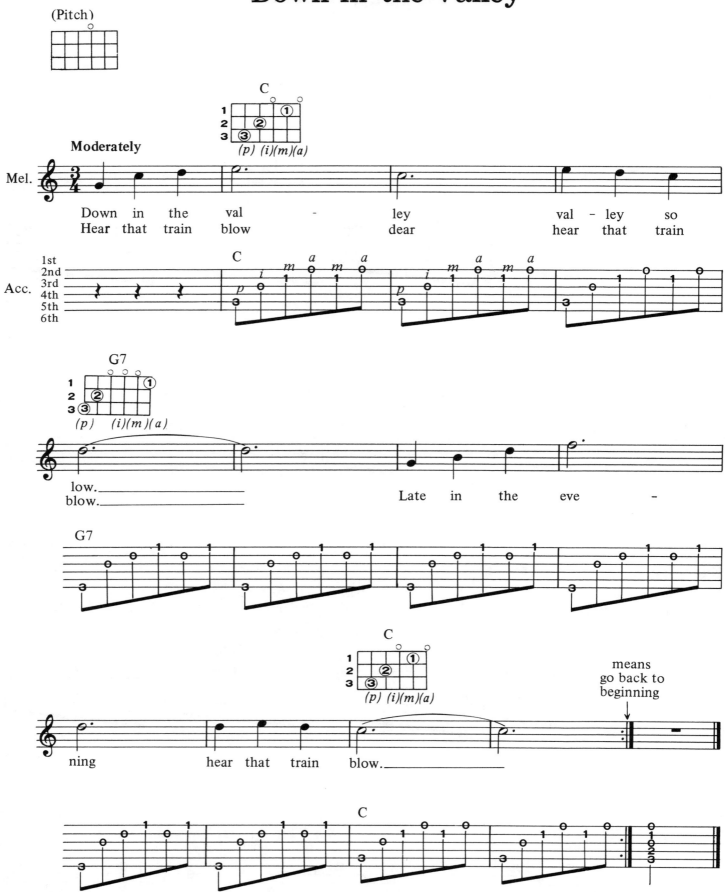

Another 3/4 Strum

Try playing the following song, Amazing Grace, with this finger pattern, (p-i-m-a-m-i). This arpeggio pattern merely has the effect of going up and coming down. It is particularly suitable for slow ballads and hymns.

Amazing Grace

Mine Eyes and My Desire

Starting Pitch

Flowing tempo
Isaac Watts

William Bay

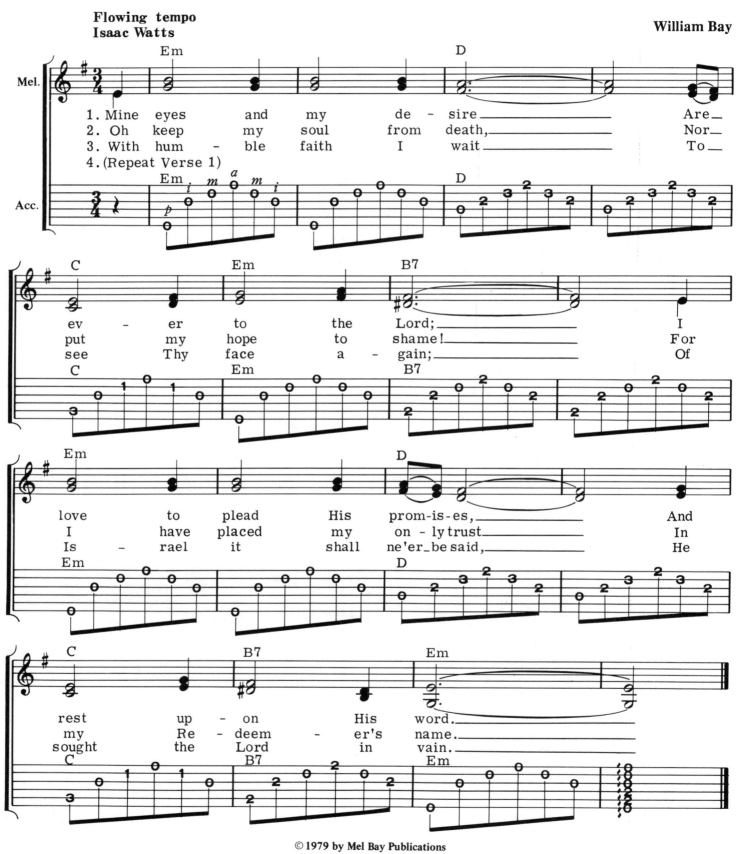

1. Mine eyes and my de - sire Are ev - er to the Lord; I love to plead His prom - is - es, And rest up - on His word.
2. Oh keep my soul from death, Nor put my hope to shame! For I have placed my on - ly trust In my Re - deem - er's name.
3. With hum - ble faith I wait To see Thy face a - gain; Of Is - rael it shall ne'er be said, He sought the Lord in vain.
4. (Repeat Verse 1)

Triplet Arpeggio

A Triplet is counted
$$\begin{bmatrix} 1 - 2 - 3, & 2 - 2 - 3, & 3 - 2 - 3, \text{ etc.} \\ \text{one-trip-let,} & \text{two-trip-let,} & \text{three-trip-let} \end{bmatrix}$$
The pattern for the

Triplet Arpeggio is   p - i - m   a - m - i

Exercise 1

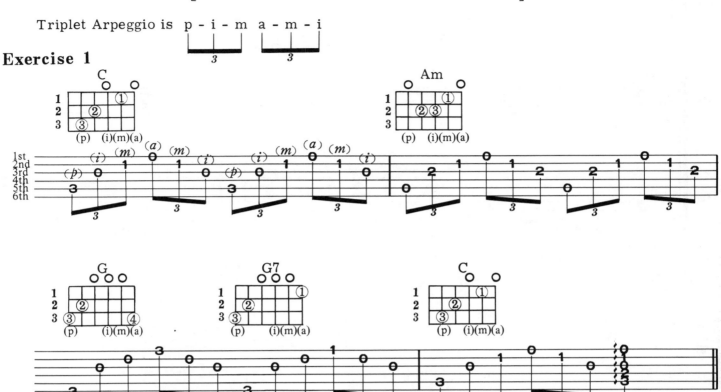

Exercise 2

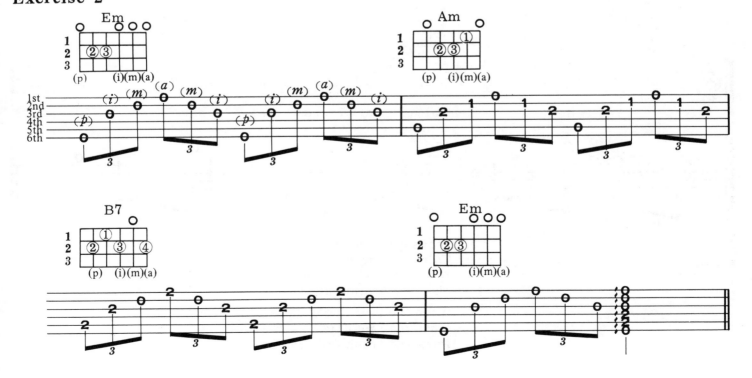

Now the Day Is Over

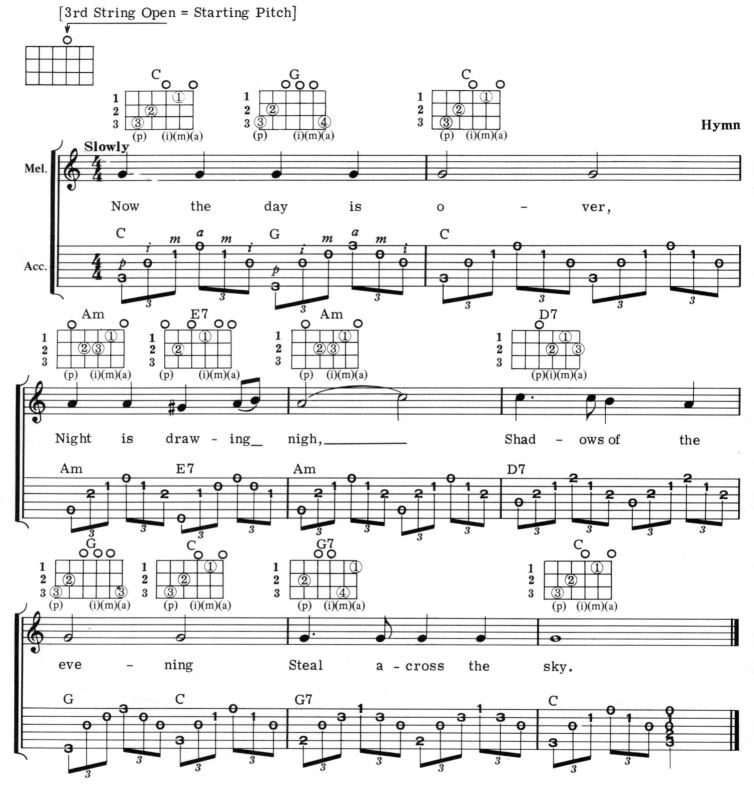

Hymn

Now the day is o - ver,

Night is draw-ing_ nigh,_____ Shad - ows of the

eve - ning Steal a - cross the sky.

2. Jesus give the weary
   Calm and sweet repose
   With the tend'rest blessing,
   May our eyelids close.

3. When the morning wakens,
   Then may we arise
   Pure and fresh and sinless,
   In Thy holy eyes.

Aura Lee

107

A New 4/4 Strum
P-i-m-i-a-i-m-i

Example 1

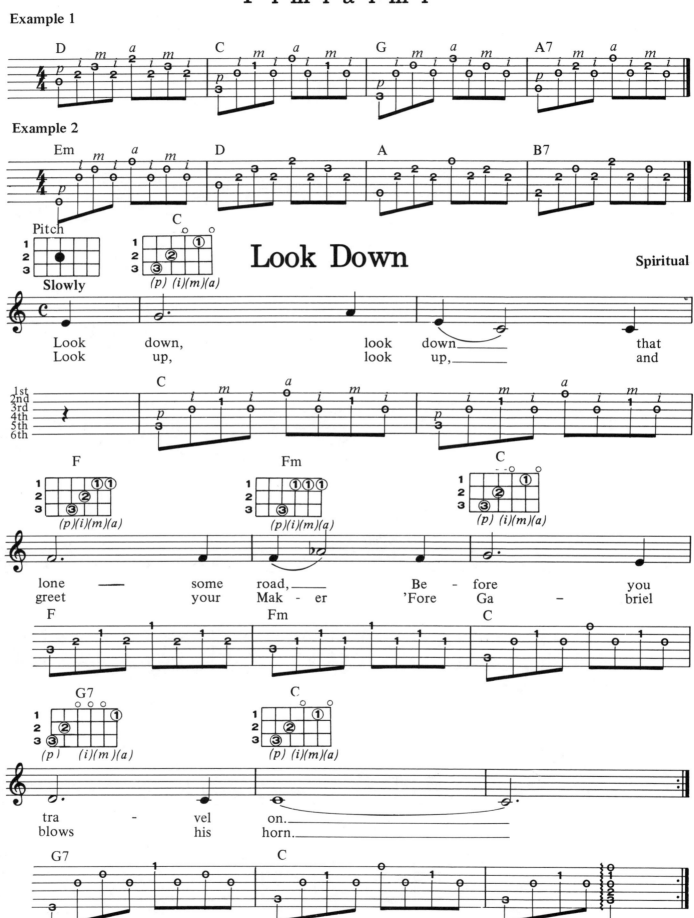

Example 2

Pitch
Slowly

Look Down

Spiritual

Look down, look down____ that
Look up, look up,____ and

lone —— some road,____ Be - fore you
greet your Mak - er 'Fore Ga - briel

tra - vel on.
blows his horn.

108

p-i-$\frac{a}{m}$-i

With this finger style effect the guitarist first plucks the bass note with the thumb. This is followed by the index finger, the middle and ring finger together, and back to the index finger. The important thing to remember is that the middle and ring fingers pluck together. Two notes should sound at once.

Bury Me Not on the Lone Prairie

Western Song

Moderately

"Oh bu - ry me not _____ on the lone prai -
In a nar - row grave _____ (a) _____ (a) _____ just six by

rie!" _____ Where coy - otes howl _____
three _____ Oh bury me not _____

_____ and the wind blows free.
_____ on the lone prai - rie."

SYNCOPATED PATTERN

This pattern accentuates the up beat of the 2nd count. It is quite common and is easy to play once you gain the basic feel of it.

Count: 1 & 2 & 3 & 4 &

Notice that 2 of the notes are tied. This means that the first note is played and the 2nd note is held.

Play Play Hold Play

Bless the Lord
(PSALM 134)

William Bay

Starting Pitch

Bless the Lord, all ser - vants of God. Lift your hands to the Lord in His sanc - tu a - ry, Bless the Lord who made heav'n and the earth.

Hammering On

Hammering On is an effect used widely in country and bluegrass picking. The player first plucks the bass note with his thumb, next he plucks the 1st, middle, and ring fingers simultaneously. Following this he raises the middle left hand finger off its string, plucks the string and while this tone is ringing he presses down the middle finger on the left hand. Finally, the 1st, middle, and ring fingers pluck their notes again simultaneously. This intersting pattern is not as complicated as it sounds. Remember that the effect is brought about largely by plucking an open string and then pressing down the left hand middle finger while the open string is still ringing.

Hammering On C Chord

Hammering On F Chord

Hammering On G Chord

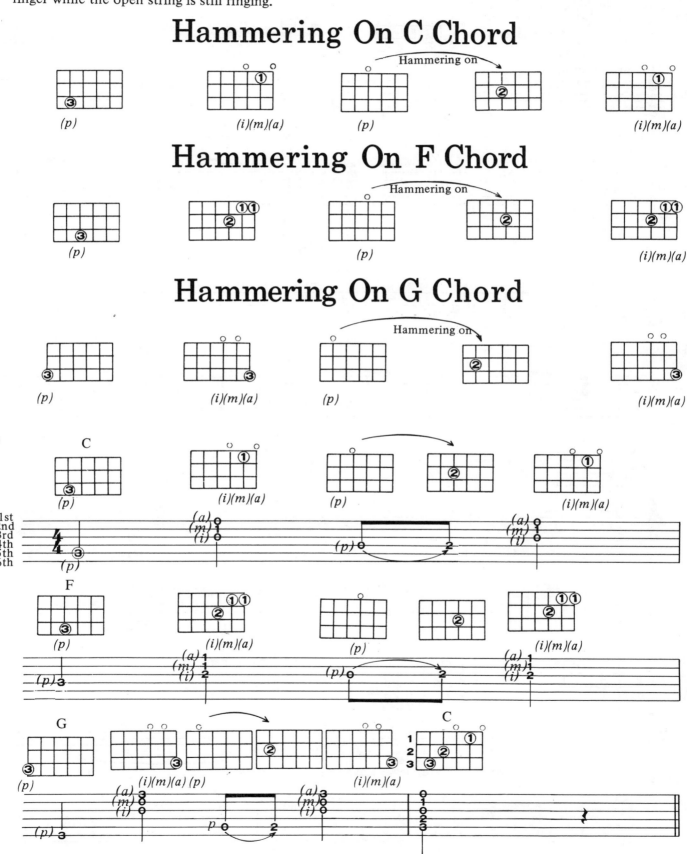

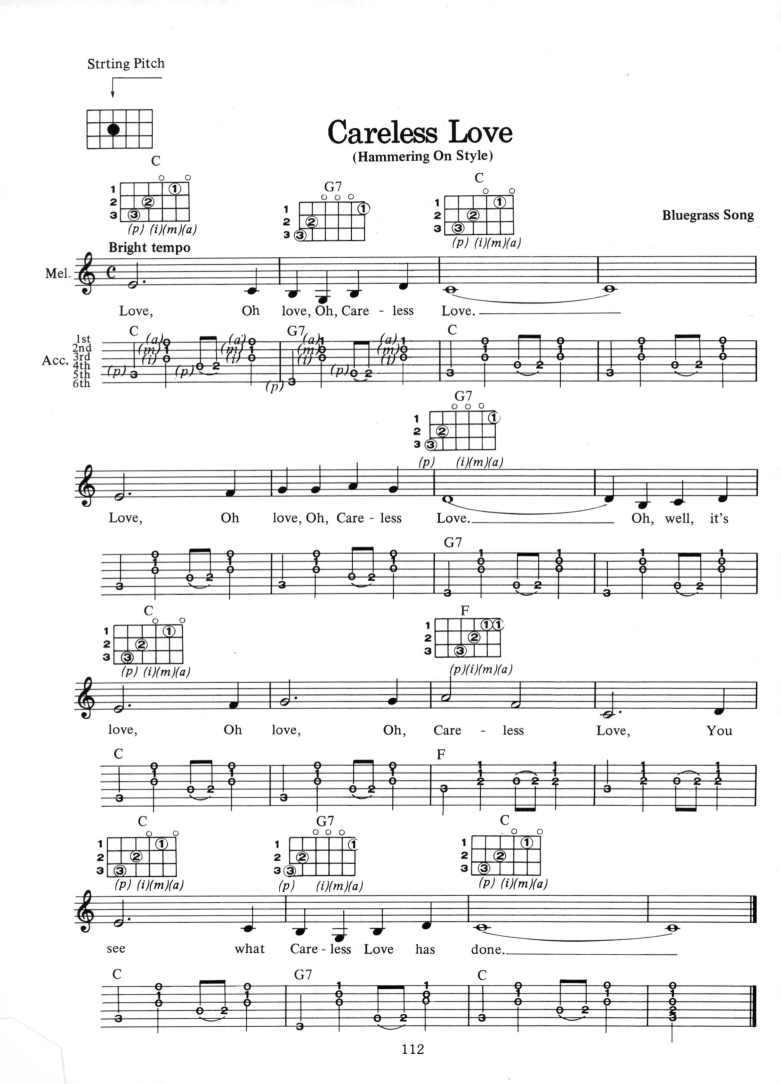

Careless Love
(Hammering On Style)

Bluegrass Song